WOMEN BL
U.S. HEALTH CA

MW00625179

WWW.WOMENLEADINGHEALTHCARE.ORG
PROMOTING *HORIZONTAL ADVANCEMENT*™

THIRD EDITION

Answering the CALL:

Understanding the Duties, Risks, and Rewards of Corporate Governance

Lynn Shapiro Snyder, Esq. and Robert D. Reif, Esq.

Created in collaboration with

darwin®

WWW.DARWINPRO.COM

FOUNDING SPONSOR

EPSTEIN BECKER & GREEN P.C.
THOUGHT LEADERS IN
HEALTH LAW®

WWW.EBGLAW.COM

Published by Women Business Leaders of the U.S. Health Care Industry Foundation, 1227 25th Street NW, Washington, DC 20037 www.womenleadinghealthcare.org

Snyder, Lynn Shapiro and Reif, Robert D., Esqs.

Answering the Call: Understanding the Duties, Risks, & Rewards of Corporate Governance (3rd Edition); Chapter Four by Chmieleski, Susan and Oard, Cynthia.

Includes bibliographical references and index.

ISBN-10: 0-9797557-0-0
ISBN-13: 978-0-9797557-0-5

Printed in the United States of America, Washington, D.C.
Third Edition

TABLE OF CONTENTS

FOREWORD TO THE THIRD EDITION

The idea for this book arose from discussions with the senior executive women involved with Women Business Leaders of the U.S. Health Care Industry Foundation (WBL). In 2002, at one of WBL's Annual Summits, we were discussing how—in light of increased scrutiny of corporate governance—we needed better information before we accepted positions as board members for a wide variety of corporations. Of course, we had heard of the Sarbanes-Oxley Act of 2002. And as busy executives, we wanted clear, concise material to inform us of the risks and to remind us of the many rewards of board membership.

Lynn Shapiro Snyder, Esq., founder of the WBL Foundation, decided to accept the challenge by authoring this book with the assistance of others. This book describes the basic information every potential (and current) board member (male or female) should know about board membership. With new laws, regulations, and reams of commentary regarding the rules, duties, and challenges of board membership being published virtually daily, attempting to capture all of this information in one place was indeed formidable. Moreover, the need to provide brief and concise overall guidance and commentary relating to some very complex aspects of board membership was challenging.

In February 2003, along with Founding Sponsor, Epstein Becker & Green, P.C., WBL published the first edition of *Answering the Call: Understanding the Duties, Risks and Rewards of Corporate Governance*. The book debuted at WBL's 2003 Summit. A complimentary copy was given to each of the nearly 100 WBL Foundation Associates attending.

Word of this book—and its usefulness—traveled quickly, and a second edition was published shortly thereafter.

To date, over *8,000* copies of this book have been made available to senior executives, directors, and potential directors at health care and non-health care companies around the globe. Its content has benefited both men and women.

In light of the rapidly evolving landscape of board membership and the overwhelmingly positive response to this book, we are now publishing a significantly expanded third edition.

This third edition also was co-authored by Lynn Shapiro Snyder, Esq., founder of the WBL Foundation and senior attorney with Epstein Becker & Green, P.C. (EBG). Joining her this time as co-author is Robert D. Reif, Esq., Chair of EBG's National Business Law Practice Group and Chair of the Corporate and Transactions subgroup within EBG's Health Care and Life Sciences practice.

This third edition includes updated summaries of the current landscape, and the latest commentary regarding director duties, risks, and rewards. It also includes the most up-to-date information on how board diversity contributes to a company's success.

Finally, we invited representatives from Darwin Professional Underwriters, a Directors & Officers insurance firm, to help us address the rapidly-changing products available for risk management in Chapter Four.

It is our hope that this third edition will help current and prospective board members make thoughtful and informed decisions.

Sincerely,

Taney Hamill
CEO
thamill@ebglaw.com

Eleanor Whitley
Director
ewhitley@ebglaw.com

August 2007

ACKNOWLEDGEMENTS FROM THE AUTHORS

Lynn Shapiro Snyder thanks Robert Reif for joining her as co-author for this third edition, as well as our Contributors, Darwin Professional Underwriters. She also thanks Eleanor Whitley, Sonja Sadowski, and Taney Hamill, each of the Women Business Leaders of the U.S. Health Care Industry Foundation, for their tremendous assistance in compiling this book. Additional thanks go to Kara Kinney Cartwright, who did a wonderful job of editing this book from cover to cover. Finally, the authors thank a significant number of other people who have helped with this endeavor over the years. They include Helen Quick, Esq., the former co-author and former EBG colleague, as well as the other EBG colleagues whose commitment and contributions to this book and its previous editions are greatly appreciated.

ACKNOWLEDGEMENTS FROM THE PUBLISHER

This book is a joint initiative by the law firm of Epstein Becker & Green, P.C. (**www.ebglaw.com**) and by the Women Business Leaders of the U.S. Health Care Industry Foundation (**www.womenleadinghealthcare.org**). On that note, WBL staff, Taney Hamill and Eleanor Whitley, would like to thank the authors of this book, Lynn Shapiro Snyder and Robert Reif, for all of their time and effort spent creating this great book that furthers WBL's mission. We also would like to thank all of those who contributed to previous editions of this book that WBL has distributed over the years. All proceeds of this book benefit WBL.

Finally, we also wish to thank Sue Chmieleski and Cindy Oard of Darwin Professional Underwriters for contributing Chapter Four.

Dear Senior Management Executive:

The pinnacle of business is a company's board of directors or board of trustees.* These directors or trustees are given important decision-making responsibilities for the company, its management, and its shareholders. These important decisions take place in any business large or small. The board of directors is a strategic asset to any business.

In small firms, the senior management and board are often one and the same. This may blur the role that a person plays in the firm. At one point, the person may be acting as management. At other points, the same person may be acting as a director. However, as firms grow, it is more likely that the board will be comprised of both inside directors, *i.e.*, senior management, and outside directors. An outside director has challenges different from inside directors whose daily jobs are from the same firm.

The current pool for outside directors from which companies can draw for corporate governance is small. It includes retired senior executives with the time and energy to be an outside director, existing senior management executives from other companies and industries, former politicians and policymakers, and anyone else who the board and management believe will be a valuable resource to the company.

Most people currently serving as board members in U.S. companies are non-minority males. As you will read in this book, diversity in the boardroom has not been achieved to date, yet there are business advantages to having a diverse board of directors. Therefore, those of you who otherwise qualify to be a director and who are "diverse" board candidates should seriously consider embracing directorship opportunities. Those who already enjoy directorships should seriously consider embracing new board candidates who provide increased diversity to the boardroom.

---

* In some entities, *e.g.*, limited liability companies, the governing body may be referred to as the Board of Managers. The terms "directors" or "trustees" refer to those individuals who have responsibility for the overall direction of the enterprise.

As a senior management executive, you have spent many years advancing your business and professional objectives. Often you have sold a product or service, you have addressed human resource issues, and you may have even bought or sold all or part of your business. You recognize that the accumulation of these experiences has value to those operating similar or even different businesses. You decide that you are ready for the task of being an outside director for another firm to help that company grow and prosper. In the event such an opportunity arises, what will be the duties, risks, and rewards involved? What type of due diligence should you do before accepting such a directorship? If you accept the directorship, what will be expected of you?

The purpose of this book is to address these basic questions briefly to help senior executives become more informed outside directors. This book is particularly designed to help senior executives decide which board positions to accept and, once accepted, how to be more effective board members.

Whether the company is for profit or non-profit, public or privately held, large or small, any decision to join a board requires a certain amount of due diligence. Also, each senior executive who is contemplating such a career opportunity should be prepared to satisfy the obligations expected from this position.

Hopefully, this book will help you in "Answering the Call."

> Sincerely,
>
> Lynn Shapiro Snyder, Founder
>
> Women Business Leaders of the U.S. Health Care Industry Foundation, and
>
> Health Care & Life Sciences Practice Leader,
>
> Epstein Becker & Green, P.C. Washington, D.C.
>
> August 2007

EXECUTIVE SUMMARY

What are the rewards for serving as an outside director?

Although there often is tangible compensation for an outside directorship, most outside directors will say that the greatest rewards for serving on a board are the intangible benefits from having the opportunity to work with the other directors of the company. The other directors are likely to be similarly situated senior people from industry who may be in a position to improve your current business or to facilitate professional growth. The camaraderie that develops through the board meeting process is very rewarding.

The other reward often mentioned is the opportunity to help another company improve based upon your guidance and experiences. There is great personal satisfaction in being able "to advise" instead of "to do" in helping a business prosper.

Then, of course, there often is compensation for a director's time and effort. There also is reimbursement for travel to board meetings. There may be a fee paid for each meeting. There also may be payment in stock or in stock options for agreeing to be a director.

What are some of the risks for serving as an outside director?

As with anything that has significant rewards, there also are risks involved in serving as a director. If things go bad there is risk to reputation. There also is risk of personal liability for something involving the company and the director. As you will read below, a director may be named in a lawsuit against the company and others. Furthermore, recently enacted legislation and heightened government scrutiny have complicated the risk analysis for certain companies. However, being sued and being held liable are two separate matters. Despite the picture painted by recent headlines, a director still rarely is held personally liable for anything involving the company unless he or she also was personally involved in the wrongful conduct.

Nevertheless, it is not a pleasant thing to be named in a lawsuit and, in light of the fact that the United States is a litigious society, a prospective director needs to know about the risks of such potential liability and about risk management tools used in the event of lawsuits, such as indemnification and insurance for directors and officers of the company.

What type of due diligence should you do before accepting a directorship?

It used to be the case that a senior executive asked to be on a board was so grateful for the honor that he or she would just say "yes." Those days are probably over. Just as the company's senior management and current board members go through a due diligence process to determine whether to extend an offer for a directorship to a particular board candidate, so, too, should the candidate ask some questions and do some of his or her own investigations to make sure there is a desirable match. This is so important because a directorship requires a very close and personal relationship amongst directors and with senior management with whom there will be a lot of interaction.

Once on the board, what will be expected from you?

Much of this book addresses the topic of what will be expected from you as a director of a company. There are certain duties and responsibilities. The bottom line is that if you decide to become a director and are given the opportunity to do so, then you must take this commitment seriously and fulfill the various fiduciary duties which are described briefly in this book.

CHAPTER ONE

Why Should a Busy Executive Want to Serve on a Company's Board of Directors?

The Women Business Leaders of the U.S. Health Care Industry Foundation (WBL Foundation) asked WBL Foundation Associates to describe the benefits they derived from holding board positions. These senior executive women overwhelmingly responded that they greatly benefited from their experiences as board members.

Foundation Associates identified business benefits such as increased opportunities for networking, visibility, and influence. They gave specific examples of the professional benefits of board membership, including:

+ *Networking, networking, networking.*

+ *Expanded my understanding of other organizations, professionals.*

+ *Opportunity to translate business initiatives to current work practice.*

+ *Worked with smart people on problems outside my field.*

+ *Got the chance to have professional growth at the governance level.*

+ *Further developed my business and leadership skills.*

+ *Has made me a much more effective CEO.*

✦ *My board memberships have allowed me to brush up on strategic planning skills.*

✦ *Gave me the opportunity to better understand the dynamics of group decision-making.*

Describing the professional benefits of board membership, as follows, Davina Lane, a director of a health care company at the time, summarized her experience:

> *My board experiences provide another dimension to my business life. I have met people in segments of business that I would not have met in the normal course of my own work. I find them stimulating and their ideas force me to look at issues from different perspectives. Serving on boards has sharpened my skills in areas not used in the ordinary course of my day.*

The Foundation Associates also described personal benefits of board membership:

✦ *Getting satisfaction and doing a good job for someone.*

✦ *Personal pride in being asked.*

✦ *Meet bright interesting people.*

✦ *Community visibility...ability to influence change.*

✦ *Affirm[ed] my desire to contribute beyond my business/ company.*

✦ *Being given the chance to influence the direction of a company that was experiencing significant market and financial challenges.*

✦ *Being a director has provided me with great contacts, new knowledge, and above all, the opportunity to make a real contribution.*

✦ *Receiving financial rewards.*

Said Sandra Van Trease, president of a St. Louis-based hospital system and director of a Fortune 500 Company:

> *Outside board participation enhances my ability to think strategically, objectively analyze courses of action, and engage in dynamic discussions which ultimately influence the direction the organization takes—it's exhilarating!*

In addition to these intangible professional and personal rewards of sitting on a board, directors may obtain tangible financial rewards. In its 2005 Public Company Governance Survey, the National Association of Corporate Directors (NACD) reported that the average annual retainer for directors ranged from approximately $19,535 to $46,321 per year, depending on the size of the company. The NACD also found that the most common retainer was $40,000 and that the average retainer for all companies surveyed was $37,250.[1]

In addition to annual retainers, board members may receive additional fees to attend meetings, to sit on a committee, and to reimburse travel expenses to and from board meetings. Furthermore, companies may offer equity and cash compensation. Equity compensation typically takes the form of stock options, but also may include direct grants of stock.[2]

Even in light of the considerable financial benefits that serving on a board can offer, Dorothy Light and Katie Pushor, in their book *Into the Boardroom*, reported something interesting:

> The results of our research on the reward side of the boardroom equation surprised us. Of course, we expected to hear directors talk about making great connections or cashing in their options for a bundle. And in some cases substantial financial rewards did occur. But after all those interviews, the widespread conclusion that emerged was this: The most apparent reward for board service is professional, the most overrated is financial, and the most lasting reward was personal.[3]

So remember, there are both tangible and intangible rewards for serving as an outside director of a company. Your challenges are first determining which board positions to accept, and then effectively serving those boards.

CHAPTER TWO

What Are a Director's Duties and Responsibilities?

Board service is—plain and simple—a commitment. In any committed relationship, each party has a responsibility to stay true to the promises of that relationship. In the company-board relationship, board members should be prepared to:

+ become educated on the rules that govern the relationship;

+ perform to their best abilities in accordance with best practices;

+ prepare for, attend, and participate meaningfully at every meeting; and

+ uphold their fiduciary duties owed to the company.

What is the role of the board of directors?

First and foremost, the board's role is to promote the best interests of the corporation. Shareholders expect the board to provide general direction for the management of the corporation's business, to be involved in major corporate decisions, and to bear the ultimate responsibility for the company's business and affairs.

A corporation's shareholders rely upon the board members to ensure that the company meets its responsibilities. Board members have the ultimate power and responsibility to determine the company's success or failure. Board members have a duty to others invested in the company—management, shareholders, lenders, and in some cases, the public.

To keep the board's power and duty in check, states have imposed "fiduciary duties"—or legal responsibilities—on board members.

What's on the agenda for a "typical" board meeting?

✦ Authorizing major corporate actions

✦ Hiring and evaluating the CEO

✦ Ensuring effective corporate auditing procedures (including retention of outside auditors)

✦ Reviewing the effectiveness of major operating and financial plans

✦ Advising senior management on operations and financial management

✦ Adopting corporate conduct policies and monitoring corporate compliance

✦ Conducting a self-evaluation—how effective is the board and its composition?

Boards also may call special meetings to act on important matters such as mergers, acquisitions, major financing, joint ventures, or divestitures.

What is a fiduciary duty?

A fiduciary duty is a legal duty imposed on individuals in positions of trust or confidence. These legal obligations, usually imposed on board members by state statute, case law, or both, require that these individuals, the "fiduciaries," act primarily on behalf of the interests *of the company*. Board members are

Directors serving on boards of non-profit corporations also have a fiduciary duty. See Chapter Eight for a discussion of fiduciary duties in the non-profit context.

required to put the company's interests above personal interests, always exhibiting loyalty, honesty, and good faith.

A board member is expected to act "(1) in good faith and (2) in a manner [he or she] reasonably believes to be in the best interests of the corporation."[4] In legal terms, these two expectations are known as the "fiduciary duty of care" and the "fiduciary duty of loyalty," respectively. Together, these two distinct duties comprise the board member's fiduciary duty.

The Duty of Care: What does it mean to act in "good faith?"

The duty of care requires a board member to treat her tasks with a certain standard of care. *Specifically, the board member should approach her duties with the level of care that another person in a similar position would reasonably believe appropriate in similar situations.*[5]

This means that a board member must be careful, responsible, and thoughtful in the performance of her duties. She must exercise common sense to make informed decisions.

Surprisingly, some board members overlook this aspect of their duty of care—they do not know anything about the company's industry. While a board member need not be an avowed expert on all facets of the business, she should have, at the very least, a knowledge base that allows her to discern whether an effective reporting system is in place. That reporting system should facilitate board oversight by providing the board with periodic and timely reports of

> Since Congress enacted the Sarbanes Oxley Act in 2002, companies increasingly are seeking directors with accounting and financial analysis skills. This requirement is often particular to certain board members who serve on the company's audit committee. Nevertheless, all board members may rely on the advice of qualified legal and financial advisors to some extent.[7] See Chapters Five and Six for a detailed discussion of this topic.

significant corporate developments from management and the company's legal and financial advisors. These reporting processes also should allow a director to evaluate management's performance independently.

Board members may rely on the advice of qualified legal and financial advisors to fulfill their duty of care.[6] Nonetheless, board members should possess a basic understanding of:

+ the principal operational and financial plans, strategies, and objectives of the company, including the operating metrics used to measure the company's performance;

+ the results of operations and financial condition of the company and its significant business segments for recent periods; and

+ the standing of the company's significant business segments relative to the company's competitors.

The Duty of Loyalty: What Does It Mean to Act in the Best Interest of the Company?

As the corporation often is owned either by persons other than management or persons in addition to management, board members must be loyal to the interests of the ultimate stakeholders of the enterprise—the shareholders. A board member must consider this duty of loyalty when faced with differing interests of stakeholder groups, including the employees, suppliers, customers, officers, and community of the corporation. The board serves as the ultimate check that the company is acting in the long-term best interest of the shareholders, although sometimes, in certain circumstances, the board must consider other non-shareholder groups, too.

No amount of pressure from the media, pleading from company employees, or even pressure from the CEO who recruited the director should sway that director from his or her primary fiduciary responsibility to act in loyalty to the best interests of the company and ultimately its shareholders.

The duty of loyalty also prohibits a board member from using his or her position as a director of the company to make a personal profit or to take other personal advantage, such as by usurping a business opportunity or advantage available to the company. Questions surrounding a board member's duty of loyalty most often arise in situations where there are potential conflicts of interest and/or corporate opportunities.

Conflicts of Interest and Corporate Opportunities

A "conflict of interest" arises when a board member, directly or indirectly, has a financial or personal interest in a contract or transaction brought before the board. A conflict of interest often arises when a director has an interest in another company with which the company proposes to merge or acquire.

Similarly, if a potential "corporate opportunity" arises that could benefit either the company or a board member (personally), the duty of loyalty generally provides that board members make the business opportunity available to the company first. Only after the company has rejected that opportunity may board members pursue it for their own or another's account.

The duty of loyalty does not necessarily forbid transactions that may involve a conflict of interest or corporate opportunity. Instead, the duty of loyalty dictates that board members either refrain from participating in the decision-making process or take other actions to ensure that the board's decision-making process is free from any consideration outside of the company's best interests.

To avoid conflicts, most companies now require that a certain number of board members be independent of the company. The definition of "independent" varies from company to company, but typically starts with the independent director not being a company employee or a relative of an employee. Indeed, current law may require independent board members under certain circumstances.

Example of a Conflict of Interest

Kristen is a board member of a coffee dispensing company. The company wants to acquire a paper company so that the coffee company no longer has to purchase paper cups from an outside vendor. In fact, the coffee company is considering acquiring a paper company owned by Kristen.

As a "conflicted" board member, Kristen's duty of loyalty requires that she and the coffee company take certain actions before any decisions are made. After Kristen affirmatively discloses the conflict, the coffee company board may decide to appoint a special committee of disinterested directors to evaluate the transaction independently on behalf of the board.

To Do List: How Can a Board Member Fulfill His or Her Fiduciary Duties?

+ Attend all board and committee meetings (if appointed to a board committee).

+ Participate actively in discussions, ask questions before and during board meetings to understand as fully as possible all potential issues, and vote on matters brought before the board for action.

+ Inquire into potential issues when alerted by circumstances.

+ As a full board or committee, discuss matters with the company's legal and financial advisors when necessary to make an informed decision; do not hesitate to employ the assistance of independent experts on any issue that calls for significant expertise or a second opinion.

+ Stay informed by reviewing board and committee meeting agendas and materials in advance of meetings.

✦ Assess independence frequently, evaluating whether other board seats or personal or business relationships could affect current and potential transactions; if necessary, inform the board.

✦ Stay current by attending educational forums on corporate governance.

✦ Get up to speed on industry and company knowledge, by diligently reviewing:

  ✧ All available annual and quarterly reports and press releases;

  ✧ Operational and financial results of the company and its significant business units—this year's, last year's, and far enough back for comfort;

  ✧ Strategic plans (both operational and financial);

  ✧ Operating metrics used to measure the company's performance;

  ✧ The relative standing of the company's significant business segments in relation to the industry competitors; and

  ✧ Risky business areas, and the extent to which the company has an effective corporate compliance program.

CHAPTER THREE

What Are the Risks of Serving on a Board?

A sweeping glance at news headlines shows that board membership does not come without risks. Between the corporate scandals and the ever-changing rules, board members' duties have come under enhanced focus—as evidenced by the increasing the number of lawsuits and government investigations into board actions.[8] These days, board of director membership presents the potential for personal civil, and even criminal, liability.

On the other hand, the actual incidence of personal liability resulting in out-of-pocket personal payments by a board member is exceedingly rare.[9] Nevertheless, board members should review a number of failings for which they may be held personally liable.

What Laws Put Board Members at Risk?

A multitude of laws and regulations put directors at risk, and familiarity with these laws is the first step in avoiding personal liability. Directors can be personally liable for any breach in their fiduciary duties to the corporation or for any breach of other various laws relating to the corporation, its behavior, and its securities. If not careful and diligent, board members can find themselves writing personal checks to the company, its shareholders, or even the government. The following attempts to outline many of the different types of laws that fall under a director's purview.

Breach of Fiduciary Duty: Directors Can Be Held Liable to Shareholders

A shareholder suit, also known as a "derivative action," is when shareholders sue the corporation as a means of "enforcing the corporation's own rights."[10] The corporation, itself, fails to sue, and so these shareholders sue in the name of (or on behalf of) the corporation. As discussed earlier, board members owe various fiduciary duties to their corporation and to its shareholders. Most shareholder suits are brought by shareholders alleging that board members or officers breached these duties. If a judge or jury finds that a director breached his or her fiduciary duties to the corporation, the director may be personally liable directly to the corporation. This means the director may have to return any personally realized profits from any "prohibited transactions" and compensate the corporation for any losses.[11]

What can constitute a breach of fiduciary duty? For starters, failure to disclose a conflict of interest, either direct or indirect, can constitute a breach of fiduciary duty. A word of caution: Even if a board member acts in good faith and fulfills his or her fiduciary duties, courts will closely scrutinize transactions where board members are self-interested.

Most derivative action suits occur based upon alleged breach of the duty of loyalty aspect, rather than the duty of care aspect of fiduciary duty. This is because it is usually much easier to prove that a board member violated the duty of loyalty. To prove a violation of the duty of loyalty, one need only verify that procedures were not followed when there was a self-interested transaction. So, to protect oneself against "duty of loyalty" derivative actions, one simply should be certain that the proper procedures always are followed.

However, to determine whether there was a breach of the duty of care, the courts must determine what a director in a similar position reasonably would believe appropriate, the "business judgment rule."

The Business Judgment Rule

The same laws that impose fiduciary duties on board members also provide protections. One of these protections is known as the business judgment rule–which comes into play in most cases involving an alleged breach of the duty of loyalty.

Most of the time, before a matter involving board conduct even ends up in court, the shareholders must make a demand that the board of directors enforce the corporation's rights that they would be suing to enforce. In other words, the board must be given an opportunity to heed the shareholders wishes.[12]

If a matter involving board conduct *does* end up in court, the business judgment rule creates a presumption that (assuming corporate formalities have been met and conflicts of interest are absent) board members fulfilled their fiduciary duty. The presumption is that board members acted on an informed basis, in good faith, and in honest belief that the action taken was in the best interests of the corporation. Essentially, if a board decision was incorrect, but if, in the process of reaching that decision, the directors exercised reasonable due diligence under the circumstances, then courts generally will uphold the board's decisions and not hold the directors personally liable. This is the case even when such a decision may have resulted in an unfavorable outcome for the company.

To find directors liable for breaching the duty of care, the business judgment rule requires evidence that the director's conduct was motivated either by an actual intent to do harm or an intentional disregard of duty. The significance of the business judgment rule is that it places the burden of finding such evidence on the shareholders.[13] Even evidence of gross negligence may not be sufficient to support a finding of personal liability against board members.

Prospective board members should note that, despite the protection of the business judgment rule, in a very small minority of cases courts have found board members personally liable

See Chapter Four for a discussion of how indemnification and insurance address these and other liability risks.

for violating their duty of care—when there was an obvious, prolonged, or egregious failure to diligently participate, oversee, or supervise, for example.[14]

As a result of such cases and the consequences suffered by corporations and their shareholders, the United States Sentencing Commission has developed stricter guidelines for effective compliance and ethics programs, and placed significantly greater responsibilities upon boards of directors.[15]

In-Depth Look at the Duty of Care and the Business Judgment Rule

One of the landmark shareholder suits took place in 1996 in the health care industry—*Caremark International Inc. Derivative Litigation*.[16] Caremark shareholders brought an action against the directors of the company after the company pled guilty to criminal charges and paid hundreds of millions of dollars in fines to the federal government for violation of health care fraud and abuse laws. The shareholders brought derivative action against Caremark's board members, alleging that the board members had breached their fiduciary duty of care and therefore should be reimburse the company for the fines. The court dismissed the shareholders' claims. In short, the court found that even though the action or inaction of the board of directors may have contributed to the corporation's troubles, the board satisfied its duty of care by, among other things, implementing programs designed to educate employees and adopting internal audit procedures designed to achieve compliance.

continued on page 25

In-Depth Look at the Duty of Care and the Business Judgment Rule

continued from page 24

In its opinion, the court articulated the director's role within a company and the limits of a director's personal liability for corporate misdeeds:

> [The Court is] of the view that a director's obligation includes a duty to attempt in good faith to assure that a corporate information and reporting system, which the board concludes is adequate, exists, and that failure to do so under some circumstances may, in theory at least, render a director [personally] liable for losses caused by noncompliance with applicable legal standards....[17] Obviously the level of detail that is appropriate for such an information system is a question of business judgment.[18]

> But it is important that the board exercise a good faith judgment that the corporation's information and reporting system is in concept and design adequate to assure the board that appropriate information will come to its attention in a timely manner as a matter of ordinary operations, so that it may satisfy its [monitoring] responsibility.[19]

> The liability that eventuated in this instance was huge. But the fact that it resulted from a violation of criminal law alone does not create a breach of fiduciary duty by directors. The record at this stage does not support the conclusion that the [director] defendants either lacked good faith in the exercise of their monitoring responsibilities or consciously permitted a known violation of law by the corporation to occur.[20]

continued on page 26

In-Depth Look at the Duty of Care and the Business Judgment Rule

continued from page 25

In the wake of *Caremark*, implementing and updating a rigorous corporate compliance program has become one of the best risk management tools against director personal liability in a derivative suit.

In 2005, the highly publicized Walt Disney Company shareholder derivative litigation[21] placed the business judgment rule back in the spotlight. In *Walt Disney*, the Delaware Chancery Court evaluated directors' responsibilities with respect to executive compensation decisions. The shareholders questioned the board's processes and decisions related to hiring Michael Ovitz as President, claiming that the enormous severance package Mr. Ovitz received upon termination of his short, and by all accounts extremely disappointing, tenure resulted from directors' and officers' inactions and conflicts of interest. The shareholders argued that the alleged misconduct constituted a breach of these directors' and officers' duties of good faith and loyalty.

While the court found that many aspects of the directors' conduct fell significantly short of corporate best practices (and offered some potential best practices), the court unanimously found that the directors had *not* breached their fiduciary duties of good faith and loyalty. Significantly, the decision specifies that, even where a director may have been negligent, the director remains protected by the business judgment rule standard because, as previously mentioned, the business judgment rule presumes that directors act in good faith. To illustrate, the court established several categories of behavior that may constitute bad faith, namely,

continued on page 27

In-Depth Look at the Duty of Care and the Business Judgment Rule

continued from page 26

(1) conduct motivated by an actual intent to do harm;

(2) actions that are grossly negligent, accompanied by certain aggravating factors (noting that gross negligence, alone, may not be sufficient to establish a breach of the fiduciary duty of good faith); or

(3) conduct demonstrating an intentional disregard for duty.[22]

Many have called the *Walt Disney* case a fundamental reassurance to directors that "actions taken in good faith and in an honest belief that the corporation's interests are thereby served comply with Delaware law, regardless of the post-hoc result."[23]

An In-Depth Look at Securities Laws: the 1933 Act and the 1934 Act

The Securities Act of 1933 was signed into law by President Franklin Delano Roosevelt, partly in response to the stock market crash of 1929. The law's two objectives are:

1. to be sure that all pertinent financial and other company information makes its way to the consumer, or potential consumer (the stock owner); and

2. to prevent misrepresentation and other fraud in the sale of securities."[24]

continued on page 28

An In-Depth Look at Securities Laws: the 1933 Act and the 1934 Act

continued from page 27

In 1934, Congress established the Securities and Exchange Commission (SEC) with the enactment of the Securities Exchange Act of 1934. The 1934 Act gave the SEC authority to regulate, discipline, and oversee "all aspects of the securities industry," including brokerage firms, transfer agents, clearing agencies, as well as the nation's securities self regulatory organizations (SROs). SROs include the different stock exchanges (example: the New York Stock Exchange) and those companies that operate them (example: the National Association of Securities Dealers, which operates NASDAQ).[25]

The 1934 Act gave the SEC power to regulate certain behavior by companies, and to "require periodic reporting by companies with publicly traded securities."[26] The reporting takes place via Form 10-Ks (the Annual Reports), Form 10-Qs (the Quarterly Reports), and Form 8-Ks (the Significant Event Reports), among others.

Both the 1933 Act and the 1934 Act have provisions relating to the obligations of directors. These provisions primarily focus on director stock ownership and disclosure. The liability exposure of a board member under a particular securities law can depend upon whether the board member is an inside or outside director, the degree of control over the corporation exercised by the board member, and whether the board member owns stock in the corporation.[27] Thus, where a director owns stock, the greater the hands-on role of the director (as an insider rather than uninterested director), the greater the risk.

Securities Laws: Directors Must Report Individual Investments (Section 16)

It is not a conflict of interest, but rather a best practice, for a board member to own securities of that board's company.[28] Once a director owns the company's securities, however, he or she is then responsible for complying with securities laws. (This applies to both private and public companies.)

For public company directors who own securities, additional rules apply. Section 16 of the Securities Exchange Act of 1934 was designed to expose insider trading. The concept behind Section 16 was that a select group of insiders would be privy to important, non-public information by the very nature of their positions, and the Section sought to "take the profits out of a class of transactions in which the possibility of abuse was believed to be intolerably great."[29]

> As Section 16 has been a newsworthy and notorious governance pitfall, potential directors may be wondering whether they can purchase directors & officers (D&O) insurance policies against the costs and exposure relating to violations of Section 16 and various laws. In most cases, however, companies are not allowed, by law to indemnify directors against federal securities law violations.[32] See Chapter Four for a detailed discussion of D&O policies.

Accordingly, Section 16 requires directors of a public company to report their holdings periodically and to report all trades. Sometimes Section 16 requires directors to return "short swing" profits to the company (*i.e.*, profits derived simply because of the timing between a sale and a purchase). Furthermore, the Sarbanes-Oxley Act of 2002 shortened the time frames for reporting certain acts under Section 16.[30]

In addition to returning short swing profits, board members can be personally liable for violations of Section 16. If the SEC or a court finds that a director has disclosed non-public information or has used such information improperly, a director may 1) be asked to pay civil penalties, 2) be banned from further service on public company boards, and, 3) even have to serve a prison term.[31]

Although companies generally help their directors and officers comply with Section 16, compliance is ultimately the director's responsibility. Accordingly, directors should seek assistance to ensure compliance with these rules, possibly including outside legal advice.

Securities Laws: Directors Must Report Corporate Information

In addition to shedding light on individual investments, securities laws also are aimed at ensuring accurate and proper disclosure of information about the corporation. This concept goes back to the origins of the 1933 Act and the 1934 Act where, in the wake of the stock market crash and on the heels of prevalent securities fraud of the 1920s, Congress adopted a system that requires companies to disclose all the necessary information in an organized format, so that individual investors can draw their own conclusions on the merits of any particular investment. This system of "full disclosure" to the investors was reinforced by the Sarbanes-Oxley Act of 2002.

Board members can protect against personal liability under securities disclosure laws in several ways. The SEC or a court typically will not hold a board member liable for violations involving disclosures if the member can prove that, after reasonable investigation, there was no reason to believe that the company made a false or improper disclosure.[33] The more diligent a director is in making sure that the proper information reaches the public, the less likely the director will face liability for the company's failing to disclose material information.

Such diligent actions include:

+ avoiding conflict of interests;

+ becoming and remaining educated about the company;

✦ making sure the reporting systems are working; and

✦ challenging management.

Laws Concerning Dividend Payments: Directors Must Distribute Payments Lawfully

Directors are the governing body that pays dividends on behalf of the corporation. Directors may be found personally liable if they approve a distribution of dividends that is in violation of the company's articles of incorporation, is in violation of legal limits placed upon dividend distribution, or makes a company insolvent.[34] Before declaring a dividend, directors may want to determine whether in-house legal counsel, financial officers, and ultimately the Audit Committee have reviewed all applicable laws and governing documents, as well as the corporation's financial statements. Directors should note, however, that they "cannot escape personal liability...by delegating to an executive committee the discretion to declare dividends."[35]

Environmental Laws: Directors Must Be Alert to Corporate Compliance

As shareholders and communities become increasingly knowledgeable and sophisticated in their understanding of environmental compliance, board members should consider their role in this regard. Two primary sources of environmental regulation are the Clean Water Act of 1972[36] and Superfund (CERCLA), enacted in 1980.[37] These statutes generated a significant increase in federal and state regulation of activities that affect the environment, as well as a greater emphasis on board members' role in corporate environmental violations. While most environmental laws make some type of direct participation by board members a prerequisite to liability, courts increasingly are willing to hold board members both civilly and criminally liable for violations. However, board members must actively participate by "having directed, ordered, ratified, approved, consented, or sanctioned the conduct."[38]

Further, authorizing a "cover-up" also may result in director liability–maybe not under the realm of environmental law, but under another aspect of fiduciary duty, such as securities law. Consider the directors of Exxon. These board members were not sued directly under environmental laws for the Valdez spill, but they did face several securities claims alleging that they were responsible for cover-ups relating to the Valdez spill.[39] [Note: the outcome of the security claims is still pending.]

Tax Laws: Directors Must Be Sure the Corporation Complies

Tax law is another area where directors must be diligent in ensuring the corporation's compliance. The board members are liable for penalties related to failure to pay both FICA and federal income withholding taxes of a corporation.[40] One way to monitor compliance in this area is to request frequent company reports on the timely payment of these taxes. In the case of a non-profit corporation, directors who approve an "excess benefit" transaction and who have not satisfied the requirements for the "rebuttable presumption of reasonable-ness" of such transactions may be subject to excise tax penal-ties.[41] See Chapter Eight for more detail on these standards for non-profit corporations.

ERISA: Directors Must Take Fiduciary Responsibility for Benefits Administration

The Employee Retirement Income Security Act of 1974 (ERISA)[42] "is a federal law that sets minimum standards for most voluntarily established pension, and health and welfare plans in private industry to provide protection for individuals in these plans."[43] The law includes responsibilities for anyone who has discretionary authority over these plans—and this includes board members.[44] Breaches of the ERISA fiduciary duty may create personal liability for directors—directors who breach an ERISA fiduciary duty may be required to restore monetary losses to the ERISA plan, or face criminal penalties.[45] Any director agreeing to take on ERISA responsibility should seek counsel and guidance on all of ERISA's complex rules, regulations, and resultant duties and obligations.

Can Directors Go to Jail?

In an article published by *Corporate Board Member* in 2002, John R. Engen interviewed several legal experts on the topic of whether directors realistically would be facing the possibility of actual jail time in the wake of all the enforcement activity resulting from highly publicized corporate scandals monopolizing the headlines at that time.[46] Mr. Engen reported that Stephen Cutler, then the SEC's enforcement director, told securities lawyers that he was eager to "heighten the personal accountability of officers and directors who elect to place their own interests ahead of those of the company and its shareholders."[47]

Despite these fighting words from the SEC chief enforcement officer, legal experts report that the likelihood that an outside director will actually go to jail for misconduct "are virtually nil." The jail time reported in the media often relates to officers who also are inside directors. A white-collar criminal defense attorney interviewed by Mr. Engen reinforced this view by stating that, in his opinion "criminal responsibility is personal," and "unless an independent director is personally involved in the illegal activity, they won't be charged."[48]

The Corporate Fraud Task Force, established by President Bush in 2002, has the mission of investigating corporate fraud, including violations of the duty of care and duty of loyalty by directors. As charges have been brought, however, many of these criminal cases have fallen apart.[49] More often than jail time, the criminal indictments of directors have led to large financial settlements.

Furthermore, criminal charges require proof beyond a reasonable doubt, which is a difficult evidentiary standard for a prosecutor to meet. This may be one of the reasons that so few people go to jail for SEC violations. In particular, TRAC, a tracking service operated by Syracuse University, reported that from 1992 through 2001, only approximately one third of the 609 potential cases referred to Department of Justice by the SEC were actually prosecuted and, of those, only 87 defendants ended up serving jail time.[50]

What Is the Risk for Out-of-Pocket Director Liability?

Unfortunately, there is no simple way to track directors' personal liability payments that are not otherwise reimbursed (such as by D&O insurance or under general indemnification rights against the corporation). In a *Stanford Law Review* article, however, three law professors conducted a comprehensive empirical study of the incidence and amount of out-of-pocket liability imposed on outside directors. The authors reviewed news stories, case law, and professional and business journals. They made hundreds of phone call interviews to law firm attorneys, in-house attorneys, D&O insurers, and current and former SEC officials to collect data during the period from 1980 through the end of 2005.[51] The study found lawsuits common and trials unusual. As for the cases that settled, the article found that "plaintiffs often recover cash, but the cash nearly always comes from the company, a D&O insurer, a major shareholder or another third party. Outside directors make personal payments in a *tiny* percentage of cases"—thirteen to be exact.[52]

These findings make a very strong case that without willful and knowing conduct on the part of a director, directors are not likely to have out-of-pocket liability even where they are personally liable. Specifically, the authors found:

> [I]f a company has a D&O policy with appropriate coverage and sensible limits, outside directors will be potentially liable to out-of-pocket liability only when (1) the company is insolvent and the expected damage award exceeds those limits, (2) the case includes a substantial claim under section 11 of

the Securities Act [of 1933] or an unusually strong section 10(b) claim [under the Securities Exchange Act of 1934], *and* (3) there is an alignment between outside directors' or other defendants culpability and their wealth. Absent facts that fit or approach this "perfect-storm" scenario, directors with state-of-the-art insurance policies face little out-of-pocket liability risk, and even in a perfect storm they may not face out of pocket liability.[53]

In Sum: How Can Directors Best Counter the Risk?

Be a conscientious director. Directors who pay attention to board proceedings, who ask questions of the management of the company in appropriate circumstances, and who generally follow best practices will decrease the chances, if not eliminate the possibility, of *"having the big job land [them] in the big house."*[54]

The real risk to a conscientious director serving a board that becomes embroiled in a law suit or a company involved in a scandal is not the possible dollars out-of-pocket, but, more significantly, the potential "time, aggravation and potential harm to reputation that a law suit can entail."[55]

To mitigate that risk, which is real and distinct, a director need only perform the requisite due diligence on a company before agreeing to serve on its board, and, once there, insist that the board follow and embrace as many of the best practices as is practicable and reasonable for the particular company and the particular board. For a detailed discussion of the due diligence techniques and current best practices for boards, see Chapter Eleven.

CHAPTER FOUR

How Can Directors Manage the Risk of Liability?

Chapter Authors:

Susan Chmieleski, Vice President, Risk Management and Client Services, and Cynthia Oard, Vice President, Health Care Underwriting, Darwin Professional Underwriters, Inc.*

As described earlier, directors may be subject to personal liability under a wide array of laws. In light of this fact and to promote individual board service, most states' laws permit companies to adopt charter provisions that limit a board member's personal liability for his or her corporate board service—through indemnification against specified legal exposures. Companies also commonly procure directors and officers liability (D&O) insurance to provide additional protection when the company's funds are not adequate to provide the financial protection allowed under state law or charter indemnification provisions.

Indemnification provisions and D&O insurance policies come in innumerable variations and provide varying degrees of protection. Before accepting any board position, a candidate should scrupulously review both to ensure sufficient protection. Thoughtfully crafted indemnification provisions combined

---

* The opinions in this chapter represent those of Susan Chmieleski and Cynthia Oard, chapter authors. They do not necessarily represent the opinions of Darwin Professional Underwriters, or any of the Darwin companies.

with a comprehensive D&O policy can go a long way toward insulating a director from using personal assets to pay a judgment in a lawsuit or government investigation.

Indemnification

Although state laws vary, both the Model Business Corporation Act and the Delaware General Corporation Law allow companies to eliminate or limit—indemnify— a director's personal liabilities to the company or the shareholders for monetary damages arising from certain breaches of the directors' fiduciary duties.[56] The Model Business Nonprofit Corporation Act, which often forms the basis for state laws on this subject, includes similar provisions.

Indemnification is not a "get out of jail free card," however. Public policy dictates that a company may not indemnify directors for certain breaches. A company's indemnification generally is *not* available to a director in the case of:

✦ Intentional misconduct;

✦ Unlawful payment of dividends;

✦ Transactions where the director derived an improper personal benefit;[57] or

✦ Insolvency of the organization or lack of resources.

Individual states may require companies to provide a minimum level of indemnification for directors, then allow companies to choose whether to provide an additional permissible level of protection. When evaluating a board position, potential directors should review the company's articles of incorporation and bylaws to ensure they provide:

✦ Indemnification as broad as state law permits;

✦ *Required* rather than *permitted* indemnification for board members. (This provides a greater guarantee and removes ambiguity as to when it will apply);

+ A provision that shifts the burden of proof to the company to prove that the directors and officers are not entitled to the indemnification, rather than requiring directors or officers prove that they are entitled;

+ A right to appeal the company's decisions related to the scope of indemnification; and

+ Advancement of defense costs, so that the expense of litigation does not drain the personal assets of a director named in a company-related lawsuit.

D&O Insurance Policies

Indemnification is essential to attracting and maintaining board members. The company's obligation to protect its directors and officers should not stop at indemnification, but should include an effective risk transfer mechanism such as an insurance policy.

D&O Insurance has its roots in the 1930s, when Lloyds of London introduced the coverage to address personal liability exposure for directors because, at that time, corporations were not legally permitted to indemnify officers and directors.[58] In order to induce directors to sit on their boards, corporations purchased D&O coverage insurance policies on behalf of their directors and officers. As this coverage provided an additional level of comfort, D&O Insurance often was referred to as "sleep insurance."[59]

Up until the 1960s, directors, officers, and their companies did not perceive a serious risk for personal liability arising from corporate activities. Consequently, D&O insurance was not prevalent. The tide turned in the 1960s as courts began to recognize the potential personal legal liability of directors and officers; D&O Insurance now is seen as an essential component of any company's risk management platform.[60] Indeed, a recent study estimated that 99% of companies today purchase some degree of protection via D&O insurance.[61]

The cost of D&O insurance is cyclical, increasing or decreasing with changes in the legal climate. In the wake of corporate scandals and significant litigation in early 2000, most companies experienced significant increases in their D&O insurance premiums. While "companies with solid finances were reporting increases in the 25% to 40% range" during 2002 and 2003, "financially precarious companies [saw] premium increases as high as 300% to 400%."[62]

Since then, insurance market pricing has stabilized. In 2004, D&O pricing actually began to decrease. Some commentators attribute this decrease to new federal laws restricting class actions, as well as to compliance provisions in the Sarbanes-Oxley Act of 2002. As companies have increased their compliance activities in the wake of these new requirements, the number of securities actions filed against directors and officers has declined. Incremental D&O premium price decreases occurred from 2004 to 2006.[63] In 2006, fewer security class actions were filed than since 1996.[64] Early 2007 reports indicate a continuation of these downward trends.[65]

However, the personal liability risks have not been eliminated. Trends show that regulators increasingly are targeting outside directors. United States government scrutiny of foreign corporations and boards is increasing as well. Shareholders are showing greater interest in executive compensation.[66] An active merger and acquisition environment poses particular risks for directors and officers—putting at risk their personal wealth unless their company maintains adequate indemnification provisions and proper D&O coverage. Consequently, directors should inquire whether the company's D&O policy contains a level of protection commensurate with that of companies of similar size and position in similar industries.

Breaking It Down—The Basics of D&O Coverage

D&O insurance coverage protects directors and officers against liability arising from their actions as directors and officers. Although each policy is different, and there are numerous D&O products to choose from, most policies consist of a few basic components:

+ A-Side Coverage,

+ B-Side Coverage,

+ Entity Coverage (or C-Side Coverage), and

+ Employment Practices Liability (EPL) Coverage.[67]

Prospective board members should review policy endorsements and exclusions that further expand or limit the coverage. Exclusions will differ from policy to policy, and in certain cases, exclusions can be eliminated with the payment of additional premiums.[68]

Board members also should look for D&O insurance policy enhancements that can reduce the risk of personal financial liability. This could include provisions specifying the handling of defense costs and order of payment, as well as dedicated A-Side policies.

All three of these policy elements—coverage, exclusions, and enhancements—are described below.

A-Side Coverage

> Wrongful act committed by an insured *person*
>
> Insurance company to pay on behalf of the insured *person*

The A-Side policy provision typically covers directors and officers when either (a) the wrongful act alleged cannot be indemnified under state law or (b) the claim is identifiable but cannot be covered by the corporation's available financial resources. As with any insurance policy, the specific definitions of these insurance terms of art, such as "loss," "claims," and "wrongful acts" will define the scope of the coverage. Each word is important. For example, the policy's definition of wrongful act will explain exactly what kind of conduct would be deemed covered.

To ensure that a policy provides adequate protection, many advisors recommend that the policy's definition of "wrongful act" be as broad as possible to "include intentional and unintentional acts, errors, and omissions (including statements made) in the discharge of a director's duties, as well as any breaches of director's duties to the corporation." In addition, directors should pay careful attention to the definition of the term "loss" to determine if it covers everything for which the director could be held liable, including attorney's fees, statutory damages, double and treble damages, arbitration awards, and defense costs. In most cases, insurance does not cover those penalties or other payments resulting from criminal acts on the part of the director.[69]

While A-Side coverage is part of the standard D&O policy, additional protection can be afforded directors and officers through what is called a "dedicated A-Side Policy." This type of policy may be purchased in conjunction with standard D&O coverage. Dedicated A-Side policies are discussed later in this chapter.

B-Side Coverage

> Wrongful act committed by an insured *person*
>
> Insurance company to pay on behalf of the insured *entity*

This policy provision insures the corporation, itself, in the event that the corporation is called upon to indemnify any or all of its officers and directors. This policy provision does not insure the corporation against its own liability, however.

Entity Coverage (C-Side Coverage)

> Wrongful act committed by an insured *entity*
>
> Insurance company to pay on behalf of the insured *entity*

This is the third piece of the puzzle. Entity coverage (also known as C-Side coverage) covers the corporation, itself, for claims made against the corporation. Claims of this nature usually are made against public corporations in connection with securities fraud. Some C-Side provisions afford coverage only when the directors and officers *and* the entity are sued. Other policies provide coverage to the company regardless of whether the directors and officers are named as defendants in the same lawsuit.

Employment Practices Liability (EPL) Coverage

Policies with EPL coverage specifically cover claims relating to employment-related issues of:

✦ harassment, including sexual or non-sexual harassment, or creation of a hostile work environment;

✦ discrimination based on race, color, religion, age, sex, national origin, disability, pregnancy, medical condition, sexual orientation or preference, military status, or other status protected pursuant to federal, state or local statute, or ordinance;

✦ wrongful termination, demotion, or failure to promote in violation of law or against public policy;

✦ breach of an implied agreement to continue employment;

✦ retaliatory treatment against an employee; and

✦ employment-related misrepresentation, negligent evaluation, wrongful discipline, or wrongful deprivation of career opportunity.

As an extension of EPL coverage, some insurance companies offer coverage for third party employment practices liability. This type of coverage insures against claims brought by third parties, such as customers or vendors, for allegations of sexual harassment or discrimination based on interactions with employees of the insured company. Typically, insurers offer this coverage at an additional premium charge.

Dishonesty Exclusion

D&O insurance is not intended to cover claims based on deliberate or willful violations of the law, fraud, or dishonesty. (This is also true in the case of corporate indemnity of a director or officer). Generally, these exclusions are modified by a clause stating that the knowledge of one director will not be imputed to another director for the purpose of determining whether coverage is available. This is called "severability." Further, most dishonesty exclusions have an "adjudication clause," which states that the exclusion does not apply absent an official finding of fraud or dishonesty, whether by admission, final adjudication, or judgment—including settlement.[70]

Insured vs. Insured Exclusion

This provision excludes coverage when one director or officer sues either another executive or the company, as well as when the company sues its own executives. This exclusion prevents a company from orchestrating a suit against its directors and officers to collect insurance proceeds. To assure the greatest amount of protection, this exclusion should be amended so it does not apply to:

+ any cross-claim, third party claim, or other claim for contribution or indemnity by an insured person;

+ any derivative action by a security holder;

+ any claim for employment practices;

✦ any claim by an insured person whose relationship with the company was terminated more than four years ago; or

✦ any claim brought on behalf of the company in bankruptcy by the company's examiner, trustee, receiver, liquidator, or rehabilitator.

ERISA Exclusion

To the extent that a director also acts as a fiduciary under a pension, profit sharing, or employee benefit plan maintained for the corporation on whose board he or she sits, the D&O policy will not insure for any liability under the Employee Retirement Income Security Act of 1974 (ERISA). ERISA can be a source of personal liability for these directors, so they should consider seeking separate fiduciary liability coverage.

Prior Acts Exclusion

This provision bars insurance coverage for wrongful acts that occurred prior to a specified time period—usually coinciding with termination of coverage under a previous policy or change in control of the corporation. Where this is a concern, most corporations will purchase "tail" coverage to cover any claims that are covered under the old policy but not under the new policy.

Professional Liability Exclusion

This provision bars coverage for liability associated with professional services. For example, if a doctor is the president of a professional corporation, the D&O coverage would not insure the doctor for malpractice claims. This distinction seems obvious. In practice, however, the distinction between acts performed in a professional capacity and those within the purview of a corporation's officers and directors may be subtle. In the health care industry, professional liability exclusions commonly disallow exposures such as medical malpractice and managed care errors and omissions. Prospective board members should consider whether they have purchased adequate coverage for those exposures separately.

Bodily Injury, Property Damage, Environmental Exclusions

This provision bars bodily injury and property damage claims. For example, an executive's insurance might cover a shareholder claim relating to environmental compliance issues, but exclude claims brought by property owners or regulators for damages resulting from the underlying environmental claim.

Defense Costs

Most D&O policies cover defense costs and liabilities. Policies differ, however, on which circumstances require the insurer to cover defense costs and when these defense costs must be paid. For example, some policies specify whether the costs should be advanced as they are incurred, or whether they should be reimbursed at the end of the process.

D&O insurers have a strong financial interest in making certain that insured directors and officers are vigorously and well defended. This suggests that the insurer would want to be involved in management of the claim. In certain circumstances, however, such as where intentional misconduct is alleged, the case ultimately may constitute an excluded claim not covered by the D&O policy. In these circumstances, early involvement of the insurer may not be warranted. The dilemma for the insurer is that it may be difficult or impossible to determine whether the claim is excluded from coverage until the ultimate resolution of the case. As a solution, most policies require the insurer to advance the costs of the defense at the outset and during the case. If the case is excluded from coverage in the end, the director or the company may be required to reimburse the insurer.[71]

Defense costs can be quite expensive. As described earlier, there are chances of being sued. Prospective board members should ensure that the company's D&O policy expressly requires the insurer to advance defense costs. The company also may want to avoid any requirement for any security or collateral delivered to the insurer in return for advancing defense costs.

Punitive Damages

Although most policies exclude fines and penalties from loss, policies deal with punitive damages in a variety of ways. Policies may cover punitive damages, exclude them along with fines and penalties, or expressly state that punitive damages are not part of a "loss."

Not all states permit insurers to cover punitive damages. State law may allow full insurance coverage, prohibit coverage, or authorize coverage for vicarious liability only. To avail themselves of the broadest interpretation available, prospective board members should request the enhancement of "Most Favorable Venue." This provision requires the insurer to evaluate the state or location when determining the extent to which punitive damages are insurable, thus expanding the potential for coverage of punitive damages.

Order of Payment

Historically, D&O policies protected the directors and officers of a company. As the D&O policy has evolved in market segments such as health care, it has come to cover a broader range of entities—the organization, trustees, committee members, managers, volunteers, and employees. As settlements rise and litigation continues, competition for the limits of the D&O policy intensifies. Directors and officers might find themselves without the coverage they need to protect their personal assets if numerous parties are named in a suit, the policy limits are insufficient to satisfy the settlement, and indemnification is not available.

The "Order of Payment" clause protects directors and officers and assures them that the company's obligation to indemnify the directors is a recognized priority. This clause, where legally permissible, provides that the personal protection of A-Side coverage shall have priority over claims under the entity protection of B-Side and C-Side coverage.

Dedicated A-Side Policy

This type of D&O policy provides directors and officers with personal asset protection when indemnification and insurance are not available or when the limits of the underlying policies are exhausted. As described above, there often are numerous parties competing for recovery under the same D&O policy. Directors and officers can add an additional line of defense dedicated solely to them through the purchase of a dedicated A-Side D&O Policy. This coverage is purely for the directors and officers of the company. It does not provide any coverage for the company, nor does it provide coverage to other insured persons who may be covered in the primary policy.

Dedicated A-Side coverage typically is purchased as a top layer excess limit that sits above all the D&O coverage limits; dedicated A-Side limits are in addition to the traditional D&O policy A-Side limits, or in the event that the B-side or C-side entity coverage limits are exhausted. The Dedicated A-Side Policy would respond with dedicated coverage available only for the directors and officers. Another benefit of the dedicated A-Side Policy is that its policy limits are protected from being frozen or seized as an asset of the company in bankruptcy proceedings, because the company is not an insured—this D&O policy is not considered a corporate asset.

In addition, an enhancement to the dedicated A-Side policy may increase its value and the commensurate protection it offers the directors and officers. A feature called the "DIC (difference in coverage) drop down" extends broader coverage for non-indemnifiable loss. The DIC drop down has fewer exclusions and often is non-rescindable by the insurance company. This A-Side DIC policy preserves coverage when the primary policy does not respond, when the organization cannot indemnify, when it denies indemnification, when underlying limits have been exhausted, or when broader terms have been negotiated for the directors and officers.

Purchasing D&O Insurance Policies

Board members should consider seeking expert advice when preparing a D&O insurance application. The law in some states supports the D&O insurance company in a denial of coverage when there has been a material misrepresentation of facts in the application. Beyond that, directors are well advised to ask questions of the auditors, management, CFO, employees, and outside experts when the company presents information about D&O insurance policies.

✦ Who is the insurance broker? Does the broker understand the company's business? Is the broker experienced in placing D&O insurance? How many insurance companies does the broker have direct access to?

✦ What insurance companies offer D&O policies? How often are carriers asked to compete for the company's policy? This is important to ensure that the best coverage is purchased at the best price.

✦ Why was one insurance company chosen rather than another? The decision should not be limited to price. Familiarize yourself with the insurance company.

  ◇ What is the financial strength of the insurance company—what is its rating from the various rating agencies?

  ◇ Has the current insurance company been a reliable partner? Has the company kept its promises?

  ◇ How long has the insurance company been in the D&O insurance marketplace? What is the insurance company's management, underwriting, and claims experience?

  ◇ Is the insurance company committed to the D&O insurance product?

✦ What are the D&O policy terms and conditions? Ask that they be listed and explained to your satisfaction.

⬧ Are the D&O policy limits adequate? Ask for benchmarking of coverage and premiums with similar companies.

⬧ It there a policy retention or deductible? If so, who is responsible for paying it?

⬧ Are there any exclusions to the D&O policy? If so, why?

⬧ Are there any sub-limits or sub-retentions in the D&O policy for certain types of exposures such as Employment Practices Liability, Antitrust, or Class Action?

⬧ Is employment practices liability coverage afforded under the policy? If not, is there a separate policy?

✦ How does the insurance company manage claims? What is its position on denying, settling, or vigorously defending claims?

⬧ What can you expect after reporting a claim?

⬧ Is there a predetermined panel of defense counsel? If so, are they experienced in defending claims against D&Os?

⬧ What are the insurance company's claim reporting requirements? How does it reserve claims?

✦ Does the carrier offer risk management assistance? Look for value added services such as board of directors liability educational resources and programs. Insurance companies also may provide invaluable assistance with employment practices risk management information and training.

Information and review of the D&O insurance policies should be part of a board's annual education. Inquire every year about any changes in insurance company, D&O policy limits, or coverage. Stay informed on all claims or potential claims under the D&O policy. The insurance broker also should provide industry information through written materials as well as live consultations.

Conclusion

Given how essential adequate D&O coverage can be for a director in this era of increased scrutiny of corporate governance, directors should seek expert advice in reviewing their D&O policy (not just the proposal from the broker, but the actual, seemingly impenetrable language of the policy, itself). Whenever a company is about to embark upon a fundamental transaction such as a merger, initial public offering, or joint venture, an expert can be instrumental in ensuring that the D&O policy is amended and expanded to an appropriate level to maintain the protection needed for the company's directors and officers. D&O policy coverage is an area where prospective and current directors need to be proactive.

CHAPTER FIVE

How Does the Sarbanes-Oxley Act Impact Directors and Boardroom Practices?

On July 30, 2002, President George W. Bush signed into law The Public Company Accounting Reform and Investor Protection Act, better known as the Sarbanes-Oxley Act of 2002—"SOX" for short.[72] Congress presented SOX to the President on July 26, 2002 after the Senate passed it by a vote of 99-0;[73] the House vote was 423-3.[74] SOX mandated one of the most far-reaching changes Congress has imposed on the public company business world since FDR's New Deal. SOX was and is an effort to prevent scandal and restore investor confidence in publicly traded companies.

An amendment to the Securities and Exchange Act of 1934, SOX technically only applies to public companies that issue stock and list their securities on a national securities exchange such as the NYSE or NASDAQ. In past several years, however, SOX has inspired similar rulemaking reforms for Self-Regulatory Organizations (SROs) such as the NYSE, NASDAQ, and non-profit organizations.

Many in the business world saw SOX as a set of new corporate governance "best practices" for all companies and their boards of directors. Whether a company's stock is publicly traded or privately held, company leaders should consider the benefits of adopting the SOX standards of governance.

SOX 101: Key Provisions

SOX is organized into eleven sections, called "titles." Prospective board members should be familiar with the requirements set forth in the titles that deal with:

1. accounting oversight,

2. auditor independence,

3. corporate accountability,

4. financial disclosures,

5. conflicts of interest,

6. fraud accountability and white collar crime penalties, and

7. whistleblower protections.

The following sections briefly describe the requirements in each of these titles.

Accounting Oversight

SOX established an oversight board, called the Public Company Accounting Oversight Board (PCAOB).[75] The PCAOB oversees the audit of public companies. Any accounting firm performing an audit of a public company must register with the PCAOB.

Auditor Independence

> See Chapter Six for an in-depth discussion of the various standards for auditor independence, and Chapter Seven for a description of the SEC's final rules on composition and responsibility of audit committees.

The indictment of a major accounting firm provided the main impetus for audit reforms. SOX aimed to eliminate conflicts of interest in audits. SOX limits what other services an accounting firm may provide to companies when the accounting firm is that company's independent auditor. SOX also mandates periodic rotation of audit partners on each account.

Corporate Accountability

SOX increases the accountability of directors, officers, and corporate legal counsel. SOX required the SEC to enact rules on reporting by attorneys employed by a corporation. Attorneys, both in-house and outside, are required to report evidence of a material violation of a securities law, a breach of fiduciary duty, or similar violation by the company to the chief legal counsel or CEO. If the chief legal counsel or the CEO does not respond appropriately, the attorney must report the incident to a committee of the board of directors comprised exclusively of outside directors.[76]

SOX requires that each annual or quarterly report filed with the SEC be accompanied by a certification by the chief executive officer *and* the chief financial officer. These certifications must include assurances of compliance with securities laws, as well as statements that the reports fairly present, in all material respects, the financial condition and operational results of the company.[77] Violators of these rules may be penalized with forfeiture of compensation for one year following any misstatement.

Financial Disclosures

SOX requires public companies to disclose in plain English—and on a rapid and current basis—information concerning material changes in their financial condition or operations. SOX shortened the filing deadline for Section 16 reports, which disclose changes in beneficial ownership, to two days.[78] Also, SOX requires the SEC to review public company disclosures at least once every three years.

How does the SEC schedule these reviews? A company's name might surface on the list for review if the company:

+ has issued material restatements of financial results,

+ has experienced significant volatility in stock price as compared with other public companies,

+ has a large market share (*i.e.*, how big is the company?),

+ is a new company with disparities in its price-to-earnings ratios (*i.e.*, the stock price is unusual given company profits), or

+ has operations significantly affecting any major sector of the economy.

Conflict of Interest

SOX requires a public company to disclose whether it has adopted a code of ethics applicable to its principal financial officer and principal accounting officer.[79] If there is no such code of ethics, the company must explain why.[80]

Fraud Accountability and White Collar Crime Penalties

SOX extended the statute of limitations for securities fraud to the earlier of (1) two years after the discovery of facts constituting the violation or (2) five years after the violation. SOX also extended the maximum prison term for securities fraud to 25 years and imposed criminal penalties for the knowing destruction, alteration, and falsification of documents in federal investigations and bankruptcy proceedings.

Among the penalties—any officer who signs an SEC certification knowing that the report is not correct may be fined up to $1 million and/or imprisoned for up to 10 years. A willful violation is punishable by a fine of up to $5 million and/or imprisonment for up to 20 years.

Whistleblower Protection

A whistleblower is an individual who lawfully provides information or assists in an investigation relating to a violation of federal securities law or securities fraud.[81] SOX provides that no company, or any of its officers, employees or contractors, may discharge, demote, suspend, threaten, harass, or in any other manner discriminate against a whistleblower.

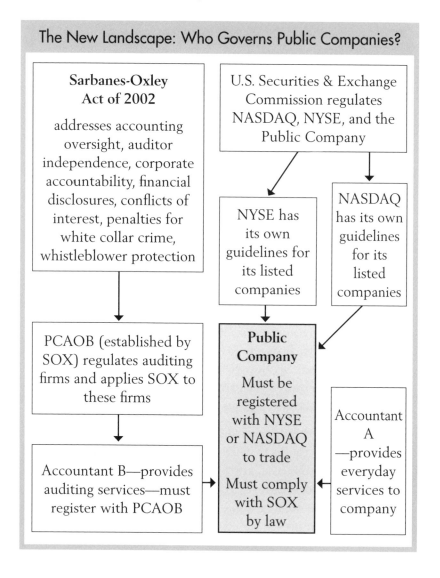

The New Landscape: Who Governs Public Companies?

Sarbanes-Oxley Act of 2002

addresses accounting oversight, auditor independence, corporate accountability, financial disclosures, conflicts of interest, penalties for white collar crime, whistleblower protection

U.S. Securities & Exchange Commission regulates NASDAQ, NYSE, and the Public Company

NYSE has its own guidelines for its listed companies

NASDAQ has its own guidelines for its listed companies

PCAOB (established by SOX) regulates auditing firms and applies SOX to these firms

Public Company

Must be registered with NYSE or NASDAQ to trade

Must comply with SOX by law

Accountant A —provides everyday services to company

Accountant B—provides auditing services—must register with PCAOB

Advanced Sox: Issues for Directors

With that backdrop, the question remains: which provisions of SOX should directors concern themselves with most? Although several provisions of SOX implicate directors' behavior and corporate governance in general, a few specific areas are of particular concern.

Be Prepared for Section 404: Internal Controls over Financial Reporting

Section 404 of SOX focuses on the efficiency of a public company's internal control over financial reporting. While many have criticized Section 404 openly, others believe that increased spending on internal controls actually will save money by pushing management to streamline operations. Collaboration among different departments and cooperation with accountants not only will enhance corporate compliance and internal controls, but also may cut costs by preventing duplicate work product and improving interdepartmental communications.

> "Ask any CEO: Section 404 of the Sarbanes-Oxley Act is the corporate equivalent of root canal."[82]

> Like most of SOX, Section 404 reports are mandatory only for public companies listed on a national exchange. There is a trend toward voluntary application to private and non-profit companies, however.[83] In the spring of 2005, a GAO report found that Section 404 costs are disproportionately high for small companies, causing some to abandon the public equity markets and go private.[84]

> In response to these concerns, the SEC announced plans to revisit some of the SOX rules, including Rule 404. On May 23, 2007, the SEC approved new guidance to help these smaller companies "strengthen their internal control over financial reporting while reducing unnecessary costs."[85] Smaller companies are slated to begin complying with Section 404 no later than calendar year 2007.

Pay Attention to Situations Involving Loans to Officers and Directors

Board members, especially those on the Compensation Committee, may want to pay particular attention to the developing law around SOX rules related to loans to officers. They may want to seek guidance from advisors. This provision of SOX could affect cashless exercise of stock options, travel advances, and even advancement of D&O expenses and defense costs—transactions previously considered ordinary.

Be Prepared to Disclose Company Information Fast

SOX requires practically a nonstop stream of information from the company to the general public.[86] What disclosures are necessary?

+ Form 10-Q (a quarterly report of financial position),

+ Form 10-K (a yearly report of financial position), and

+ Form 8-K (a report of unscheduled events or company changes, typically filed 4 days after a triggering event).

Previously, form 8K filings only included events such as bankruptcy, acquisition, or director changes. Now, companies must file Form 8K when other events occur, including entry into or termination of unusual material agreements, or the creation of a financial obligation that will not appear on the balance sheet.[87] Additionally, SOX allows companies to use Form 8K to comply with "Regulation FD"—the fair disclosure regulation. This regulation requires companies to notify the public when the company discovers a leak of non-public information.

SOX shortened the time frames for all of these filings. In response to these rules, a board, and, in particular, the committees of the Board, should begin to prepare for the time when companies will be expected to disclose much more information about financial and business changes than in the past, and do so much more quickly. Board members may want to ask management about the procedures and controls needed to comply with these new rules.

Treat Whistleblowers with Caution

SOX addresses the issue of whistleblowers as follows:

1. Companies can be delisted from national securities exchanges if they do not have procedures to receive and appropriately address employee whistleblower complaints about company accounting practices. The audit committee must oversee and closely supervise these procedures. You may be familiar with anonymous hotlines or website services that receive whistleblower complaints. These methods may be expanded, as a result of SOX, to include complaints relating to specific accounting issues.

2. Whistleblowers can file a civil suit if they believe they were wrongfully discharged, harassed, or discriminated against because of their whistleblower actions.

3. SOX makes it a felony to take harmful action against a whistleblower.[88]

Understand the Role of the Company's Lawyers

Board members should become familiar with inside and outside counsel's role with respect to the corporation and the directors. These lawyers represent the company as a legal entity—not individual directors. On many issues, the interests of the individual board members and the company are aligned; the company's lawyers, in effect, may represent the interests of the board. In other situations, however, board members may need to seek their own separate counsel to ensure that their personal interests are being served.

Lawyers are expected to report breaches and violations "up the ladder," reporting incidents to the CEO, chief legal officer, or the audit committee as necessary.

The SEC requires companies to establish a qualified legal compliance committee (QLCC). To qualify as a QLCC, a committee must include at least one member of the company's audit committee and two or more independent board members. A QLCC must adopt written procedures for receiving and resolving reports of material noncompliance.[89]

What Are the Immediate and Long Term Effects of SOX?

SOX undoubtedly has had a major impact on the operations of public boards of directors. It has begun to influence the governance practices of private company boards and non-profits' boards of trustees as well. Immediately following its enactment, SOX set off a wave of state legislative proposals which mimicked SOX on a state level.[90] While it currently appears that states will not adopt SOX-like regulations for private companies, those companies widely recognize the benefits of structuring and implementing a SOX-like compliance program.

Any conscientious director on the board of a public company should be intimately familiar with the ever-evolving SOX rules and regulations. A director on the board of any company (public or private) should keep generally informed about SOX's overall corporate governance implications. All directors should ensure that they are kept apprised of applicable state law initiatives relating to corporate governance and reporting requirements. Finally, directors should note that not all provisions of SOX became effective upon enactment in 2002. Directors should keep up to date with the interpretive rules that the SEC periodically issues.

As described in this chapter, SOX established new legal requirements. Even where those requirements do not apply, SOX has ushered in a trend toward stricter scrutiny and enforcement. Whether sitting on the board of a public, private, or non-profit company, a director always should continue to follow the basic tenets surrounding a director's fiduciary duties—the duty of care and the duty of loyalty.

CHAPTER SIX

How Do the NYSE and NASDAQ Listing Standards Shape Board Requirements?

Before the New York Stock Exchange (NYSE) was established, stockbrokers and other merchants bought and sold most securities in and around the Wall Street area of Manhattan. The NYSE traces its origins to a founding agreement on May 17, 1792 when 24 stockbrokers signed an agreement to trade with one another beneath a Buttonwood Tree outside 68 Wall Street. Today the NYSE is a thriving exchange, and part of a global for profit corporation called NYSE Euronext.[91]

In contrast, NASDAQ began trading on February 8, 1971, heralding itself as the world's first electronic stock market.[92] Unlike a floor-based exchange, NASDAQ's market makers and trading systems connect into NASDAQ from across the globe. Currently, NASDAQ boasts listing more companies and conducting more trades per day than any other U.S. market, with 3,300 listed companies.[93]

New NYSE and NASDAQ Listing Standards

Given that most U.S. public companies are listed on either the NYSE or NASDAQ, when both markets responded to SOX by proposing stricter listing standards in November 2003, they substantially changed the landscape of corporate governance for the majority of the business community.[94]

Companies listed on these exchanges immediately analyzed the new listing standards and began modifying compliance procedures, reviewing the composition of boards and committees, and searching for independent directors. Many companies had spent the previous year working toward SOX compliance; the new listing standards required added measures.

The most revolutionary of the changes were the "independence" requirements for the composition of the board and its committees. The independence requirements mandated that boards, for the first time, reach outside their Rolodexes to find independent director candidates. As one SEC Commissioner stated in a 2005 speech, "[The independence] requirement alone immediately opened seats in the Boardroom [and]...entry into the boardroom is no longer controlled by the old saying of 'it's not what you know, but who you know'...there is no question that it's now what you know that matters."[95]

While most companies have satisfied the minimum requirements for independent directors, and many companies have exceeded them, some companies still struggle to determine who is an independent director—and how "independence" differs between the NYSE and NASDAQ. Although both exchanges provide several tests, the Board ultimately must discern who is an independent director. These tests are explained in detail on the pages that follow.

NYSE vs. NASDAQ Listing Standards: Board Independence

NYSE[96]	NASDAQ[97]
General Independence Requirement	
A majority of the board must be independent.	A majority of the board must be independent.
Bright-Line Independence Tests	
The following persons would *not* be considered independent:	The following persons would *not* be considered independent:
✦ An individual, or an immediate family member who is or was an employee of the company within the last 3 years;	✦ An individual who is or was an officer or employee of the company or any subsidiary of the company within the last 3 years;
✦ An individual who received or whose immediate family has received more than $100,000 in direct compensation from the company (other than director and committee fees or deferred compensation for prior services) in any of the last 3 years;	✦ An individual who accepted, or who has a family member that accepted, payments from the company or any subsidiary of the company in excess of $60,000 during any one of the last 3 years (except for certain exempted payments);

continued on page 66

NYSE vs. NASDAQ Listing Standards: Board Independence

continued from page 65

NYSE[96]	NASDAQ[97]
Bright-Line Independence Tests (continued)	
✦ An individual who is or was, or who has an immediate family member who is or was, a current partner or employee who participates in the company's audit, assurance, or tax compliance practice of a firm that is the company's internal or external auditor within the last 3 years; ✦ An individual who is or was, or who has an immediate family member who is or was, employed, within the last three years, as an executive officer of another company where any of the company's present executive officers serves or served on such other company's compensation committee; and	✦ An individual who is a family member of an individual that is or was employed as an executive officer by the company or any affiliate of the company during the past three years; ✦ An individual who is, or has a family member who is, a partner, a controlling shareholder, or an executive officer in any organization to which the company made or from which the company received, payments for property or services in the current or any of the last three years that exceed 5% of the recipient's consolidated gross revenues for that year or $200,000, whichever is more (except for certain exempted transactions);

continued on page 67

NYSE vs. NASDAQ Listing Standards: Board Independence

continued from page 66

NYSE[96]	NASDAQ[97]
Bright-Line Independence Tests (continued)	
✦ An individual who is, or who has an immediate family member who is a current executive officer, of a company that has made payments to, or received payments from, the listed company for property or services in an amount which, in any of the last three fiscal years, exceeds the greater of $1 million, or 2% of such other company's consolidated gross revenues.	✦ An individual who is, or has a family member who is, employed as an executive officer of another entity where, at any time during the past three years, the executive officers of the company have served on such other company's compensation committee; and ✦ An individual who is or was, or has a family member who is or was, a partner or employee of the company's outside auditor *and* who worked on the company's audit anytime during the last 3 years.

continued on page 68

NYSE vs. NASDAQ Listing Standards: Board Independence

continued from page 67

NYSE[96]	NASDAQ[97]
Other General Independence Tests	
The directors of a company may determine that any individual is not independent if such individual has a material relationship with the company (either directly or as a partner, shareholder, or officer of an organization that has a relationship with the company).	The directors of a company may determine that any individual is not independent if such individual has a relationship, which, in the opinion of the board, would interfere with the exercise of independent judgment in carrying out the responsibilities of a director.

NYSE vs. NASDAQ Listing Standards: Other Governance Issues

Issue	NYSE[98]	NASDAQ[99]
Annual Certifications	Each company CEO must annually certify that he or she is not aware of any violation by the company of any NYSE corporate governance listing standards.	Each company must promptly notify NASDAQ after any executive officer becomes aware of any material non-compliance with the corporate governance standards, but there is no specific annual certification requirement.
Audit Committees	Each company must have an audit committee that satisfies Rule 10A-3 of the Securities and Exchange Act of 1934, as amended (requiring, among other things, that the audit committee be composed entirely of independent directors).	Each company must have an "all-independent" audit committee of at least three members, who have not participated in the preparation of the company's financial statements during the last three years and who have the ability to read and understand fundamental financial statements. continued on page 70

NYSE vs. NASDAQ Listing Standards: Other Governance Issues

continued from page 69

Issue	NYSE[98]	NASDAQ[99]
Audit Committees	The audit committee must have at least three members, each of whom is financially literate. The audit committee must have at least one financial expert. The audit committee must have a written charter (the standards detail specific minimum information that charter must include).	The audit committee must have at least one financial expert. A formal written audit committee charter must be adopted, and reviewed annually (the standards detail specific minimum information that the charter must include).
Code of Conduct and Governance Guidelines	Each company must adopt and disclose a code of business conduct and ethics for directors, officers, and employees and promptly disclose any waivers of the code for directors or executive officers.	Each company must adopt a code of conduct applicable to all directors, officers, and employees, and must make the code publicly available. continued on page 71

NYSE vs. NASDAQ Listing Standards: Other Governance Issues

continued from page 70

Issue	NYSE[98]	NASDAQ[99]
Code of Conduct and Governance Guidelines	Each company must adopt and disclose corporate governance guidelines. The guidelines must be posted on the company's website. The guidelines should address topics such as director qualification standards, director responsibilities, director access to management, director compensation, director orientation and continuing education, management succession, and annual performance evaluations of the board.	Each code must require that any waiver of the code for executive officers or directors be made only by the board and be disclosed to shareholders promptly.
Executive Sessions	The non-management directors must meet at regularly scheduled executive sessions without management.	The independent directors must have regularly scheduled meetings at which only independent directors are present.

continued on page 72

NYSE vs. NASDAQ Listing Standards: Other Governance Issues

continued from page 71

Issue	NYSE[98]	NASDAQ[99]
Internal Audit Function	Each company must have an internal audit function to provide management and the audit committee with ongoing assessments of the company's risk management processes and internal controls.	No similarly specific requirement.
Nominating and Compensation Committees	Companies must have a separate nominating/corporate governance committee and a compensation committee, each composed entirely of independent directors.	Not required as separate committees. The company may instead rely upon a majority of the independent directors to discharge responsibilities under the rules.

continued on page 73

NYSE vs. NASDAQ Listing Standards: Other Governance Issues

continued from page 72

Issue	NYSE[98]	NASDAQ[99]
Nominating and Compensation Committees	The nominating/corporate governance committee and the compensation committee must each have a written charter (the standards detail specific minimum information that each charter must include).	Nominees for director must be selected by a majority of the independent directors or an "all-independent" Nominating Committee. A formal written charter or resolution addressing the director nomination process must be adopted. A majority of the independent directors or an "all-independent" Compensation Committee must determine compensation of CEO and all other executive officers. The CEO may not be present during voting or deliberations.

Proof of Compliance: A Change in the Governance Landscape

Companies have been working diligently to comply with the new listing standards, as demonstrated in a variety of surveys. Consider the following:

✦ "The number of independent directors in the companies.... rose from 278 in 2001, to 443 in 2004;"[100]

✦ "Independent directors comprise 75 percent or more of the boards of 81 of the Top 100 companies, and the CEO is the only non-independent director of 35 Top 100 companies;"[101]

✦ "A total of 94 percent of all S&P 500 boards now have a lead or presiding director, compared with 85% last year. Just 36 percent reported having this position in 2003. The increase represents the strengthening board leadership by independent directors, even if not in the chairman role;"[102]

✦ "Active CEOs on average now serve on less than one outside corporate board, down from 2.0 in 1998. Active CEOs/COOs account for 32 percent of new board appointments, down from 53 percent in 2000;"[103]

✦ "20 percent of newly appointed directors are women;"[104]

✦ "A total of 98 percent of boards have identified at least one financial expert, up from 91 percent last year and 21 percent in 2003. S&P 500 companies identified 908 financial experts on 468 boards in 2005, compared with 832 in 2004 and 146 in 2003. The percentage of designated financial experts on boards has increased to 18 percent of all board members, up from three percent in 2003. A total of 48 percent of boards have identified more than one expert. It is anticipated that the number of financial experts will continue to rise;"[105] and

✦ "Board self-evaluations are rapidly becoming a 'best practice' for all public companies, not just NYSE-listed companies."[106]

To assist companies with compliance related to the new rules and SOX generally, the NYSE and NASDAQ have established orientation programs for new board members. For more information on the exchanges' new director orientation programs, visit the following websites:

✦ **http://www.boardmember.com** (for information about *Corporate Board Member* magazine's educational sessions, supported by NYSE)

✦ **http://www.nacdonline.org** (for information about the National Association of Corporate Directors programs, supported by NASDAQ)

For more detailed guidance on the NYSE and NASDAQ Governance Standards, see the following NYSE and NASDAQ websites:

✦ **www.nyse.com**

✦ **www.nasdaq.net**

Conclusion

Although SOX and the new listing standards cover much of the same ground, companies and their boards must not only be aware of the differences, but also be prepared to meet all applicable obligations. Like SOX, the new listing standards have changed what governance means for public companies. They also have created new board vacancies, and a commensurate need for independent directors with integrity and knowledge to fill them.

CHAPTER SEVEN

Are There Additional Requirements for Members of Audit Committees?

In the last few years, American media, pundits, and regulators have focused attention on one particular committee of the board of directors—the audit committee. This focus began in early 1999 with the release of the NYSE's Blue Ribbon Committee *Report on Improving the Effectiveness of Corporate Audit Committees*, which recommended a more powerful audit committee with increased obligations and duties.[107] Since then, new rules have changed the composition and the responsibilities of the audit committees as we know them.

General Roles and Responsibilities of the Audit Committee

The audit committee is an important subset of the board of directors of a corporation, especially in public companies. In general, the audit committee oversees the corporation's financial reporting. It also monitors and evaluates the company's internal and external audit processes and personnel (*i.e.*, the outside auditor). Audit committees also are called on to conduct special investigations of financial and accounting matters.

What Does an Audit Committee Typically Do?

The list of responsibilities and duties of the audit committee varies, depending upon the type, complexity, and size of the corporation. The audit committee's tasks may include:

✦ reviewing corporate annual financial statements;

✦ reviewing and monitoring corporate financial reporting procedures and internal financial controls;

✦ evaluating the performance of a corporation's external auditor;

✦ assessing and monitoring a corporation's internal audit department and the performance of executives in that department; and

✦ managing communications between the external auditor, the internal auditing executives, management, and the board of directors.

What is an Audit Committee Not Responsible For?

Contrary to popular opinion, the audit committee is not responsible for planning and conducting audits, determining the accuracy of financial statements in all material respects, or assuring the corporation's compliance with all applicable financial laws and regulations. It is the responsibility of the audit committee, however, to provide the ultimate oversight for these functions.

One of the audit committee's most important tasks is managing the corporation's relationship with the corporation's external auditors. This task includes making recommendations to retrain or replace the external auditors. The audit committee meets with the external auditors before and after the audit to discuss any special procedures necessary or problems encountered. The audit committee also reviews a letter to management from the external auditors that summarizes audit observations.

The audit committee's oversight role is entirely dependent upon the information that the committee seeks and receives from management and the internal and external auditors. Consequently, an audit committee should have direct access not only to external auditors, but also to the corporation's finance, treasury, and legal personnel. In short, the audit committee provides another viewpoint from which those board members on the committee may see what is going on inside a company. It also provides a separate pipeline of information for board members not on the committee—separate from the information submitted directly by management.

What Does an Audit Committee Look Like?

Audit committees typically consist of three to five independent directors. As outlined in the previous chapter, NYSE and NASDAQ require audit committees to consist exclusively of independent directors. In any case, members of an audit committee should be independent of management and "disinterested"—free from relationships that would interfere with the exercise of independent judgment.

Audit committee members also should (1) be financially literate and (2) have a sufficient understanding of financial reporting and monitoring principles to identify and address significant financial issues that may arise.

NYSE and NASDAQ Rules: Seeking Financial Experts

NYSE and NASDAQ require that a board member who is a "financial expert" sit on each public company's audit committee.[108] Companies must report, regularly, to the SEC whether their audit committee has at least one financial expert.

Who would qualify as a financial expert? Someone with:

+ an understanding of generally accepted accounting principles (GAAP) and financial statements;
+ experience applying GAAP in connection with creating estimates, accruals, and reserves;
+ experience preparing or auditing financial statements of generally comparable issuers;
+ experience with internal accounting controls; and
+ an understanding of audit committee functions.[109]

Who would not qualify as a financial expert? Individuals with the title CFO, CPA, or Controller are not automatically qualified as financial experts. Similarly, just because someone was never CFO, CPA, or Controller does not mean he or she is not a qualified financial expert. Rather, the NASDAQ and NYSE rules require the board of directors to take a hard look at a person's actual qualifications and experience, not just titles on a resume, to determine whether a person meets the requirements to sit on the audit committee.

An Opportunity for Financial Experts

If one does possess the required financial skills, volunteering to sit on the audit committee, referred to by some as the "hot potato job,"[110] is a very good way to gain entry to a board of directors.

For a discussion of the liability facing directors in today's enforcement and litigation climate, see Chapter Three.

According to the Investor Responsibility Research Center, in 2002 more than one quarter of large companies were required to change the composition of their audit committees to comply with the NYSE and NASDAQ rules.[111] Escalating the need, many members of audit committees are declining to seek reelection in the wake of a wave of corporate scandals.

An individual may be well-suited for service on the audit committee if he or she:

+ has the requisite experience and comfort with financial matters;

+ is versed in the financial practices of the industry in which the company operates;

+ is prepared to commit to the increased workload of an audit committee member, in addition to a director's regular responsibilities; and

+ most importantly, possesses extraordinary common sense and an attitude of constructive skepticism.[112]

The Audit Committee vs. The Corporate Compliance Committee

To manage the risk of liability, many corporations have adopted corporate compliance programs that address seven guidelines established by the U.S. Sentencing Commission.[113] If faced with noncompliance, these companies then may be able to reduce their overall liability exposure by pointing to their compliance program.

One corporate best practice calls for a subcommittee of the board to review and monitor corporate compliance program activities. As compliance issues may overlap with the responsibilities of the audit committee, companies often have the company's chief compliance officer report corporate compliance program activities to the audit committee. The audit committee often has more than enough to do, however, in the context of working with external auditors. As a result, it is becoming more common for a separate committee of the board to be tasked with corporate compliance monitoring responsibilities or to have a different standing committee of the board, for example, the governance committee, responsible for these matters.

In the health care industry, the federal Department of Health and Human Services' Office of the Inspector General has issued two papers on corporate responsibility and corporate compliance.[114] Each details the importance of having an effective corporate compliance program, as well as the role of board members as overseers. Although these papers were written for the U.S. health care industry, the concepts in these papers also apply in other industry sectors. Directors should review these papers for potential best practices.

CHAPTER EIGHT

What Additional Duties and Risks Face a Director on the Board of a Non-Profit Corporation?

Whether a company is organized as a for profit or non-profit corporation, the directors have the responsibility to promote the best interests of the corporation and to fulfill their fiduciary duties. Directors of non-profit corporations also are responsible for ensuring that the actions of the corporation further the non-profit organization's charitable mission. As a result, non-profit directors have not only a duty of loyalty and duty of care, but also a unique duty of obedience, as explained below.

What Interests Do Non-Profit Directors Serve?

Non-profit directors may be elected by existing directors, the board of a corporate member, or by the beneficiary constituency of the non-profit corporation. Identifying whose interest to serve is not as easy for non-profit directors as it is for their for profit counterparts. After all, non-profit corporations do not have shareholders. A non-profit director's fiduciary duty is owed to the corporation's best interest and to the organization's charitable mission.

Do the Definitions of Duty of Care and Duty of Loyalty Change for Non-Profits?

Like their for profit counterparts, directors of a non-profit corporation must demonstrate that they are fulfilling their duty of care—acting as a person in a similar position would reasonably act. The non-profit laws in at least twelve states, however, include additional requirements for procedures to validate "interested" transactions and the burden of proof of an interested transaction's validity.[115] In most states, the state Attorney General has the authority and responsibility to monitor and oversee charitable organizations.

The duty of loyalty takes on an additional element with non-profit corporations. Non-profit directors' duty of loyalty includes compliance with the federal tax code. The federal tax code prohibits "private inurement" (private benefit) from the activities of federal tax-exempt organizations. Specifically, no part of the earnings of a tax-exempt organization may "inure to the benefit of any private share-holder or individual."[116] If a director benefits, the director may have breached of his or her duty of loyalty. Private inurement can place the corporation's federal tax-exempt status in jeopardy as well. Moreover, as explained in Chapter Three, if a particular transaction results in an excess benefit to an "insider" (*e.g.*, in the case of compensation or other payments), a director approving that transaction could be liable for excise tax penalties, if he or she cannot meet the requirements for the rebuttable presumption of reasonableness.

> See Chapter Two for more on interested director transactions and the duty of loyalty.

A step that all boards can take to ensure compliance with the duty of loyalty is to implement a comprehensive conflict of interest policy. The Internal Revenue Service (IRS) has issued sample policies, including particular procedures to address potential conflicts of interest.[117] These policies should be part and parcel of the corporation's overall corporate compliance program. Conflicts of interest policies also should be reviewed regularly and revisited in light of the ever-changing corporate responsibility environment for all boards of directors.

Case Examples: Fiduciary Duties

One of the most famous cases addressing fiduciary duties of care in a non-profit health care context is *Queen of Angels Hospital v. Younger.*[118] In *Queen of Angels*, a hospital's Catholic sponsor claimed it was owed sixteen million dollars for past services rendered by its nuns to the hospital. The hospital board subsequently settled with the sponsor, agreeing to pay $200 per month for each nun over the age of 70, whether or not the nun had worked at the hospital. The California Court of Appeals held that the directors of the hospital breached their fiduciary duty of care because the settlement did not have a reasonable basis. The court reasoned that, although the sponsor's claim for compensation was made in good faith, the hospital board did not properly exercise its business judgement; both the sponsor and the hospital considered the services rendered by the nuns to be donations. Therefore, the hospital had no legal obligation to pay the claim. Accordingly, the hospital's board had no reasonable basis for believing in the validity of the claim and breached its fiduciary duty of care by agreeing to pay. This case illustrates that, even in a non-profit context, when determining whether directors have violated their duty of care, courts will not focus on the actual decision rendered by the board, but rather, the underlying decision-making process.

One of the seminal cases discussing fiduciary duties of loyalty for directors of non-profit corporations is *Stern v. Lucy Webb Hayes National Training School for Deaconesses & Missionaries* (known as *Sibley Hospital*).[119] In *Sibley Hospital*, plaintiffs brought a class action lawsuit against a variety of defendants, including individual trustees, alleging that members of a hospital board of trustees breached their fiduciary duties of loyalty by mismanaging hospital funds.

continued on page 86

Case Examples: Fiduciary Duties

continued from page 85

Board trustees had instructed Sibley Hospital to deposit hospital funds in non-interest bearing accounts at financial institutions in which the trustees had interests. The plaintiffs pointed to evidence demonstrating that the trustees failed to disclose those individual interests. The United States District Court for the District of Columbia held that the trustees breached their duties of care and loyalty because they were grossly negligent in failing to supervise properly the corporation's investments (the duty of care) and in engaging in self-dealing transactions (the duty of loyalty).

Despite its holding, the *Sibley Hospital* court declined to award damages incident to the injunction. Instead, the court required that each newly-elected trustee read the court's opinion and the related order, and that proof of that reading be set forth in a signed document or meeting minutes. The court also ordered that, at least a week prior to each meeting of the full board, the trustees receive a formal written statement prepared by the hospital's treasurer, disclosing in detail the full extent of all hospital business with any bank or other financial institution since the last meeting. Finally, the court ordered each trustee to disclose to the board, prior to regularly scheduled meetings, any affiliations with any bank or other financial institution.

What is the Duty of Obedience?

The duty of obedience requires the directors of a non-profit organization to remain faithful to the charitable mission and purposes of that organization. Directors will find these charitable purposes in the corporation's articles of incorporation or organizational charter.

A non-profit corporation with tax-exempt status has the responsibility of acting for the approved charitable purpose. The duty of obedience arises because donors rely on the corporation to use gifts for the corporation's stated mission. The diversion of corporation resources to other goals, even other charitable goals, is unlawful.

Some charitable activities resemble profit activities. For example, non-profit and for profit hospitals may offer the same services, serve similar populations, and even charge similar fees. However, under the Internal Revenue Code, tax-exempt hospitals must satisfy the community benefit standard, which requires that the entity justify its tax-exempt status by providing a quantifiable benefit to its community.[120]

In addition, non-profit corporations may engage in activities unrelated to the organization's charitable purpose, including commercial activities, so long as the organization is *primarily* engaged in activities that further its charitable purpose.[121] However, these unrelated business activities may result in taxable "Unrelated Business Income."[122]

Non-profit directors, with their duty of obedience, encounter a more difficult and complex decision-making process than do directors of for profit corporations, who are subject only to the duties of care and loyalty. In a merger or other business transaction, for example, it may be appropriate for the directors of a non-profit hospital to accept a lower bid from one of several suitors because the chosen bidder would provide a far higher level of public benefit or service to the community.

Case Example: The Duty of Obedience

The duty of obedience has formed the legal bases for substantial litigation involving non-profit corporations. A prime example is *In re Manhattan Eye, Ear & Throat Hospital (MEETH)*.[123] The decision in *MEETH* noted that the duty of obedience requires a director of a non-profit corporation "'[to] be faithful to the purposes and goals of the [corporation],' since 'unlike business corporations whose ultimate objective is to make money, non-profit corporations are defined by their specific objectives: perpetuation of particular activities are central to the *raison d'être* of the organization.'"[124]

What Conduct Would Breach the Duty of Obedience?

Although the answer to this question varies depending on the circumstances, the following examples illustrate the types of conduct that might constitute a breach of the duty of obedience:

+ Failure to monitor legal changes in the requirements for tax-exempt status;

+ Failure to monitor the activities of employees and agents to ensure that their actions are true to the company's charitable mission;

+ Failure to monitor the use of the corporation's funds to ensure that such funds are used to support mission; or

+ An unauthorized change or expansion of the corporation's activities outside of the corporation's stated charitable mission.

Does the Business Judgment Rule Apply to Non-Profit Corporations?

For an introduction to the business judgment rule, see Chapter Two.

The conventional wisdom is that directors of non-profit corporations enjoy certain protections against liability, including the business judgment rule, similar to that applicable to a for profit corporation. This rule creates a presumption of nonliability. If evidence demonstrates that directors met their duties of care and loyalty and took into account the corporation's charitable mission, the business judgment rule operates as shield from personal liability—even if the board's decision was not favorable to the corporation.

The rationale behind the business judgment rule is the same for both profit and non-profit corporations: it encourages rational risk-taking and innovation. It also limits litigation and unfair exposure, encourages quality directors to serve, and limits the intrusion of the judicial system into corporate governance.

What is the Risk of State Enforcement Against Non-Profit Directors?

Non-profit directors face three principal types of enforcement actions—criminal enforcement actions, civil enforcement actions, and tax assessments. Criminal prosecution generally is limited to the most egregious violations. This might include conduct similar to criminal conduct by a for profit corporation, such as egregious environmental liability, or from negligence resulting in bodily harm. Consequently, most enforcement actions for breaches of fiduciary duties by non-profit directors are civil actions seeking either damages or orders to prevent future violations.

State attorneys general have the authority to bring actions on behalf of the state to preserve the assets of charitable, non-profit corporations located in their jurisdictions. In most states, the state attorney general has either sole or primary standing to take action against directors of non-profit corporations for breaches of fiduciary duty.

Many commentators believe that the substantial increase in the number of non-profit corporations, the sophistication of their operations, and the broad manner in which they affect the public has led to a corresponding rise in recent fiduciary duty enforcement activity. It is hard to determine the extent of enforcement activities and state oversight—these proceedings generally are not public. In some cases, the state does not want these proceedings to become public as it may "chill" donations from the public to the charity. Nevertheless, it appears that litigation remains rare.

What Role Does the IRS Play in Governing Non-Profit Boards?

The IRS also may bring enforcement action against a non-profit corporation and its directors. As noted above, the benefit of tax-exempt status brings increased accountability. To obtain charity tax-exempt status, a non-profit corporation must satisfy IRS requirements. (There are tax exemptions for other types of non-profit corporations, but because of the tax exemption and deductibility of contributions, the IRS focuses scrutiny on charities.) Foremost, the organization must be organized and operated exclusively for one of the charitable purposes set forth in the Internal Revenue Code.[125] These purposes include charitable, religious, educational, scientific, literary, testing for public safety, fostering national or international amateur sports competition, and the prevention of cruelty to children or animals.[126] Failure to meet the "operation" test could result in excise tax penalties (applicable to insider economic transactions) or a loss of exemption.

To prevent private inurement, the Internal Revenue Code prohibits certain tax-exempt entities from engaging in excess benefit transactions with insiders of the organization.[127] An excess benefit transaction is a transaction where the tax-exempt organization pays more than the fair market value of the benefit it receives or transfers assets for less than the fair market value of assertion services received.[128] Typically, insiders are officers, directors, managers, or others in a position to exercise control over the exempt organization. Entities that engage in excess benefit transactions must disclose these transactions to the IRS.[129] Failing to disclose a material transaction could result in both excise taxes as well as loss of exemption.

In addition to the disclosure requirements, excess benefit transactions also may trigger intermediate sanctions. Intermediate sanctions consist of three tiers of excise taxes on the excess benefit transaction.[130] First, the disqualified person who received the excess benefit may have to pay a 25% tax on the excess benefit.[131] Second, if the excess benefit is not paid back to the tax-exempt entity within a certain time, the disqualified person also will have to pay an additional 200% tax on the excess benefit.[132] Finally, if the managers of the exempt organization knowingly approved the excess benefit transaction, they individually must pay a tax of 10% of the excess benefit.[133] Significantly, the liability for a non-profit director in an excess benefits transaction can be twofold: (1) The director could be the person who receives an excess benefit; (2) The director also could be a "manager" who knowingly approved the transaction. As noted earlier, there is risk to a director who is not a recipient of the benefit, but who approved the benefit, if the decision-making process followed certain defined procedures. These procedures include: (1) The decision-making body being free of conflicts; (2) the reliance on external data showing fair market value and (3) the contemporaneous documentation (in Minutes) of the body's actions.

How Can Non-Profit Directors Manage These Risks?

As described in Chapter Four, most states' laws permit profit and non-profit corporations to limit a board member's personal liability in order to encourage board membership. By law, the corporation may indemnify its directors and officers against certain liabilities.

These "liability shield" laws protect uncompensated non-profit directors and officers from acts or omissions committed in the scope of their duties within the non-profit corporation.[134] Moreover, even if compensated, there is available the protection afforded by D&O insurance, indemnification, and the business judgment rule.

What Sarbanes-Oxley Means for Non-profit Corporations

As non-profit corporations are not publicly traded, most provisions of the Sarbanes-Oxley Act do *not* apply to non-profit corporations. A few SOX provisions do apply—for example, those relating to the penalties for obstruction of justice.[135]

> For a detailed discussion of Sarbanes-Oxley and its implications, see Chapter Five.

Nevertheless, voluntary compliance with SOX and other federal, state, and private *SOX-like* standards can lead to significant and practical benefits. For example, a non-profit corporation that adopts SOX-like provisions may be able to procure D&O insurance at favorable terms. Non-profit organizations may face pressure to fulfill some of the SOX requirements to exhibit "good corporate governance practices." These demands and expectations may originate from a number of sources, including insurers, institutional investors, bond rating agencies, and state laws and regulations.[136]

Some SOX provisions are best practices for non-profit corporations. Enacting any of these provisions could lead to better governance, as well as increased credibility and accuracy of non-profit financial statements. See Chapter Five for specifics.

Which SOX-like provisions has the IRS instituted?

In the wake of SOX, the IRS has increased oversight of tax-exempt organizations, including emphasis on financial disclosures and conflicts of interest. The IRS is increasing scrutiny on potential new non-profits, as well as existing non-profits.

In 2004, the IRS released an updated Form 1023. This is the form non-profits use to apply for exempt status. The new form requires additional information regarding the potential non-profit organization's compensation structure, as well as its conflict of interest policy.

In 2005, the IRS issued a revised Form 990, the tax return that non-profit organizations must file each year. This form now asks non-profit organizations to list the five most highly compensated independent contractors for professional services and the five most highly compensated independent contractors for all other services. The purpose of this new requirement is to improve the agency's ability to monitor potential conflicts of interest between professional service providers and corporation insiders.

The revised form also requests a list of key employees or officers related to the tax-exempt entity—whether by business or family—as well as any key employees or officers compensated by organizations related to the non-profit. Finally, the IRS now asks non-profits to disclose deferred compensation or benefits to former officers, directors, trustees, or key employees. These new provisions aim to prevent private inurement and assure the independence and loyalty of the tax-exempt organization's insiders.

Finally, recently promulgated draft revisions to the IRS Form 990 information return are intended, in part, to apply SOX-like disclosures and certification requirements.

Conclusion

Directors of non-profit corporations should be cognizant of the unique aspects of a charitable enterprise, and well-attuned to the growing demands that non-profit corporate directors conduct themselves the way for profit corporate directors are expected to conduct themselves, with all of the attendant protections and risks.

CHAPTER NINE

Why Is Gender Diversity in the Boardroom Important and Where Are the Opportunities to Achieve It?

Chapter Authors:
Taney Hamill, CEO of the WBL Foundation and
Eleanor R. Whitley, Director of the WBL Foundation

As corporations around the globe focus on good corporate governance, it is becoming increasingly necessary for these corporations to acknowledge the enormous benefits of diversity in the boardroom. A wholly diverse boardroom is crucial to excellent corporate governance, because it allows the demographics in the boardroom to reflect "the interest of all stakeholders, including shareholders, employees, customers, suppliers, and the communities [that] the organizations impact."[137] Although many other types of diversity, including culture and ethnicity, are tremendously important, this chapter will focus on issues specifically surrounding *gender* diversity in the boardroom.

Women earn more than 57% of bachelor's degrees in the United States, more than 59% of masters degrees, and more than 48% of all doctorate degrees.[138] They enjoy "enormous clout in the market place, making 83 percent of consumer purchases and influencing over 91 percent" of these purchases.[139]

Yet, according to Catalyst, a non-profit organization dedicated to advancing women in the workplace, women hold only 14.6% of the board seats in Fortune 500 companies. Many of these seats are held by the same woman.[140] While the 14.6% statistic shows improvement from prior surveys, the picture inside the board-room remains bleak. The woman director continues to serve alone or with just one other woman.[141] Women on boards including two or fewer women experienced feelings of tokenism and stereotyping.

On the other hand, boards with *three or more* women had a noticeably different dynamic, one where gender "becomes a non-issue."[142] A 2006 report by the Wellesley Centers for Women, *Critical Mass on Corporate Boards: Why Three or More Women Enhance Governance*, described interviews and discussions with fifty women directors, twelve CEOs, and seven corporate secretaries from Fortune 1000 companies. One woman director said: "One woman is the invisibility phase; two women is the conspiracy phase; three women is mainstream."[143] Based upon these interviews and decisions, the study demonstrated that a critical mass of three or more women can cause a fundamental change in the boardroom and enhance corporate governance.

At current rates, "it will take 73 years for women to be equitably represented (50 percent) on boards."[144] There is no doubt that women are advancing–one by one–but a collision of factors are providing a true opportunity for boardroom gender diversity to increase in a meaningful way. Not only is research demonstrating that adding women to corporate boards is both practical and profitable, but boards are feeling a push, reflected in the best practices imposed or recommended by countries, large investment funds, and state governments. As SOX encourages boards to evolve and seek a more inde-pendent "candidate list," there is a real opportunity to achieve a critical mass of senior executive women in U.S. for profit corporate boardrooms.

Does Gender Diversity in the Boardroom Correlate with Shareholder Value?

> *There is a real debate between those who think we should be more diverse because it is the right thing to do and those who think we should be more diverse because it actually enhances shareholder value. Unless we get the second point across, and people believe it, we're only going to have tokenism.*

Karen J. Curtin, Former Executive Vice President, Bank of America[145]

Now more than ever, research demonstrates that representation of women or minorities on corporate boards significantly increases company profitability and improves board governance practices. Both contribute to shareholder value. A recent 2007 Catalyst study found, when looking at Return on Equity, that Fortune 500 companies with three or more women board members outperformed those [companies] with the least women on the board by 53 percent.[146] Looking beyond the Fortune 500, an Oklahoma State University study published in 2002 found the same result in Fortune 1000 firms: a significant positive return on assets when compared with companies with a low number of women on the board.[147]

How else can the financial success of diversity be measured? The 2007 Catalyst study found the return on sales and return on investments to be 42 percent and 66 percent greater, respectively, for those Fortune 500 companies with three or more women on their boards. These results—the increased return on equity, sales, and investments—were mirrored consistently across most industries.[148]

Canadian studies also have established that adding women to boards is not just "the right thing to do" but the "bright thing to do."[149] In 2002, the Conference Board of Canada measured how women affect the way boards perform. The research showed that boards not only act differently when women are present in the boardroom, but that these differences directly lead to better governance practices. By investigating the impact of women's contributions in six key areas of good governance, the Conference Board's research showed that diverse perspectives change board processes. These differences in process lead directly to differences in outcome. The diversity in viewpoint, talents, and ideals builds the business case for greater diversity in board members.[150]

Consider the following data taken from the Conference Board of Canada's report:

Organizations with Boards Including Two or More Women	Organizations with All Male Boards[151]
Board averages 2.64 of 5 accountability practices.	Board averages 1.51 of 5 accountability practices.
Board reviews 5 or more nonfinancial performance measures regularly.	Board reviews 2.5 nonfinancial performance measures regularly.
Board explicitly assumes 94% of responsibilities recommended by TSE.*	Board explicitly assumes 72% of responsibilities recommended by TSE.
Gender representation is number two selection criteria for board.	Gender representation is number nine selection criteria for board.

*TSE stands for Toronto Stock Exchange

A 2004 study of publicly traded boards by the European Corporate Governance Institute also found gender diverse boards make for more effective companies. This study found that boards with more women hold more board meetings and that the company's stock faced less variable returns.[152]

Other evidence that board gender diversity leads to better governance is anecdotal, although no less resounding. The 2006 Wellesley study found that women make a difference in three significant ways:

> "[1] the content of boardroom discussion is more likely to include the perspectives of the multiple shareholders...
>
> [2] difficult issues and problems are considerably less likely to be ignored or brushed aside which results in better decision-making...[and]
>
> [3] the boardroom dynamic is more open and collaborative."[153]

Other experts agree "a homogeneous board can be slower to recognize potential problems,"[154] and diversity "provides a richness and quality of information that you just don't have if everyone is of like mind." [155]

"Big global companies need diverse boards to understand their diverse employees, companies, and investors,"[156] and "to better represent all shareholders, nurture better appreciation of 'intangibles' like work/life issues, and [to] help recruit and retain top executive women."[157] With regard to recruitment, a lack of women on corporate boards means a lack of women in the room during recruitment and retention of the CEO and succession planning. A lack of a critical mass of women in the boardroom also results in a shortage of women as committee chairs, including Nominating Chair—a role many consider essential to true board power.[158]

A wealth of research already proves that companies with diverse top management teams produce better corporate financial performance. According to a 2004 Catalyst study, for example, companies with gender diversity in upper management experience a nearly 35% greater return on equity and a 34% greater total return to shareholders than those companies with less diverse top management teams.[159]

International Initiatives in Support of Gender Diversity in Governance

A 2004 study by Britain's Ethical Investment Research Service found that 46% of major global companies had no women on their boards. Companies based in the United States fall behind companies based in other countries with only 14.6% of women on the Fortune 500 boards. In contrast, according to recent figures, in Denmark, Norway, and Sweden, women account "for around 21% of the directors."[160]

Early steps towards equality on Norwegian corporate boards began in 1985 with a 40% requirement for women on Norway's *public* committees.[161] The dramatic increase from the 7.5% of women on Norway's boards in 2003 largely is due to a law passed in November 2003. This law mandated companies registered on the Norwegian Stock Exchange to have "at least 33-50% of each gender depending on the size of the board." Boards of over 10 members were required to have 40% of each gender in the boardroom. The law became effective on January 1, 2006 for new companies; the deadline for pre-existing companies is the end of 2007. As of January 2006, only 18% of these pre-existing companies had achieved this gender diversity requirement.[162]

In Chile, when Michele Bachelet was sworn in on March 11, 2006 as the new President of that country, she "appointed a cabinet of 10 men and 10 women, and designated the governors of the country's 12 regions on the same gender diversity basis," declaring Chile "to be the first country that will have, in public sector decision making positions, total parity" between men and women.[163]

United States Initiatives to Support Gender Diversity in the Boardroom

Although the United States has yet to enact any laws such as those in Norway, progress has come about through state and investor initiatives. In October 2002, for example, Connecticut State Treasurer Denise Nappier launched a Board Diversity Initiative, aiming to "increase the participation of women and minorities as members of Boards of Directors of Connecticut corporations."[164] The initiative, modeled after NYSE independence standards established that same year, promoted board diversity as a governance best practice. It is no surprise that Nappier's initiative successfully persuaded several companies to diversify their boards by 2003—Nappier is the "principal fiduciary of the $18 billion Connecticut Retirement Plans and Trust Funds," a major shareholder in many companies.[165] Nappier's initiative is similar to that of other investors. "TIAA-CREF, the Council of Institutional Investors, and California Public Employees' Retirement System (CalPERS) all reference board diversity in their corporate governance guidelines" as best practices.[166]

Calvert Group, Ltd., a private investor, has taken similar approaches towards board diversity. In the last ten years, Calvert has filed 38 shareholder resolutions relating to board diversity in order to encourage companies to seek diverse (in terms of both gender and ethnicity) candidates.[167] Calvert also has proposed model language for nominating corporate governance committees to assist in the nomination of diverse candidates.[168]

Survey and research results are beginning to show that these efforts are having a positive effect. Larger firms have started to recognize the benefits of gender diverse boards, with research showing more women on boards of Fortune 500 companies as compared to Fortune 1000.[169] As firms are adding independent directors, the same research shows that the more diverse the board, the more likely women are being invited into the boardroom.[170]

The Changing Board and the New Candidate

So why—if gender diversity is so good for shareholder value— would companies continue to have boards that are not more gender balanced? According to a survey by the National Association of Corporate Directors, 75% of boards do not have a plan in place to recruit more women and minorities. Yet, over 50% of respondents to that survey believed they "should have such a plan."[171]

One reason for the lack of gender diversity may be business leaders' natural instinct to surround themselves with others with whom they identify. Boards currently are mostly men, so it is their natural inclination to continue adding other men. Another reason may be the historical convention favoring a current or retired CEO for a board opening, due to that person's business experience. As most CEO positions have been occupied by non-minority men, historical convention perpetuates the drive for the same candidates.

But these boards—still mostly men—no longer have the options they had in the past. That traditional candidate pool of sitting or former CEOs is now taxed to the limit.[172] These senior executives, either out of preference or company policy, are limiting their number of board memberships. At the same time, companies often have policies that limit or bar board participation by senior management executives other than the CEO. Consequently, in their search for new "independent" directors, companies are now "looking to new sources to fill director positions"[173] such as senior vice president positions with unique expertise in areas such as information technology or human resources. The 2006 Wellesley study added, "People who claim gender blindness may appear to be driven to seek 'merit,' but they often overlook the availability of highly qualified female candidates who are not plentiful in the traditional feeder pool of Fortune 1000 CEOs."[174]

The prevailing misperception of a lack of qualified senior executive women is another reason for the delay in achieving boardroom gender diversity. "Few Fortune 1000 CEOs are women…. Boards must look beyond the obvious Fortune 1000 CEO candidate pool, [and] new processes must be established to identify highly qualified women with the skills to serve."[175] Considering these additional executive levels as potential board candidates, the pool immediately increases. In the Fortune 500, women hold only 6.7% of CEO positions, but 15.6% of *corporate officer* positions. This creates a pool of 400 potential women board candidates.[176]

In response to legislation or to poor statistics, a variety of quasi-governmental organizations have stepped in to help companies identify women board candidates. These entities have published lists that identify qualified female executives; this is one of the ways that countries such as Norway have assisted in training and preparing a supply of senior executive women to serve on corporate boards pursuant to the recent government mandate.[177]

A significant number of senior executive women in companies other than the Fortune 500 have the skill sets that could be attractive to a Fortune 1000 Nominating Committee Chair. For example, the Women Business Leaders of the U.S. Health Care Industry Foundation boasts over 1,600 senior executive women—including CEOs—and women board members from companies all over the world doing business in the U.S. health care industry. Thus, there is a robust supply of senior executive women and experienced female board members available for the Fortune 1000 boards.

Conclusion

There has been a "widespread redefinition of what consti-tutes a qualified [board] candidate,"[178] a "seismic shift," leading companies to look toward new sources to fill director positions. Senior executives who previously had little chance of being invited to join a board are now in demand.[179] Board search experts report "a greater willingness by boards to consider candidates farther down in an organization... [including] senior functional or general management executives, including chief operating officers, chief informa-tion officers, CFOs and business unit leaders."[180] Contrasting the data from the 2001 *Spencer Stuart Board Index* (SSBI) to the 2006 SSBI, one can see a new profile for directors emerge, including:

✦ *"More first time directors*—nearly one-third of all new directors last year,

✦ *More directors who are not CEOs*, but are other senior corporate executives—CEOs now comprise only 29 percent of new directors compared with 47 percent in 2001,

✦ *Greater diversity but boards still seek more*—Women comprise 15% of S&P 500 directors, compared with 12% in 2001. This year, [the SSBI] conducted additional research of the largest 200 S&P 500 companies revealing that minorities comprise only 14 percent of directors. The majority of boards [SpencerStuart] surveyed are eager to increase those numbers."[181]

According to Julie Hembrock Daum, the founder and chair of Spencer Stuart's Board Services Practice, "[w]hile it may be more work to identify and recruit directors who are not currently serving as CEOs or have prior director experience, clients find it increasingly necessary as well as worth the effort to add crucial diversity of background, experience, and skills to their board."[182] In other words, corporate boards are changing the way they have traditionally selected new board members, and that should bode well for more diverse board candidates.

Of course, such opportunity means that senior executive women (and other diversity candidates) from all segments of the economy need to "answer the call" and seek out these board positions during this unique window of opportunity. Such particular board candidates must be in charge of their own horizontal advancement.™ Chapter Ten explains what each senior executive diverse candidate can do to increase her chances of being considered for a corporate board seat.

CHAPTER TEN

How Can Women Board Candidates and Boards Find Each Other?

The challenge for a gender-diverse executive seeking entrance to corporate America's boardrooms is not a lack of credentials, but a lack of visibility—being seen as a potential candidate by nominating committees, search firms, other board members, and even the CEO or chair of one's own company. To that end, women senior executives need to make it known that they are ready, willing, and able to answer the call to serve as corporate board members.

Lynn Shapiro Snyder founded the WBL Foundation with a mission to increase the number of women on corporate boards.[183] This organization recognizes the "strong and growing" supply of senior executive women— and the particularly large number of these women active in the United States health care industry. As previously cited, WBL alone has over 1,600 senior executive women among its members, many of whom are ready, willing, and able to answer the call to serve on corporate boards. To advance its mission, WBL helps board search firms and nominating committees locate these women free of charge. Details follow later in this chapter.

How Women Can Get on the Nominating Committee's "Radar Screen"

WBL has published ten recommendations to help women establish their presence as a potential board candidate and position themselves on the Nominating Committee's radar screen. These ten recommendations are as follows:

1. **Get line experience.** Most CEOs and Nominating Committees want candidates with significant operational experience. Profit and loss responsibilities are preferable. If the candidate is in a "staff" position, that experience could include other valuable expertise, such as information systems experience, government/public policy experience, or international experience for a global marketplace.

2. **Fill in gaps in knowledge.** Not everyone in senior management today majored in business or finance in school. Consequently, there may be gaps in a candidate's educational background that act as a barrier to managing— let alone governing—at the board level. Even if a candidate did study business or finance, she may not know the most current information. To address these gaps, board candidates should consider attending executive educational programs to strengthen weak spots, especially if the weak spots are financial skills.

3. **Package yourself as a board candidate.** Prepare for board consideration, not employment consideration. Highlight not only employment and educational experience, but also operational credentials, proven results, crisis management skills, industry knowledge, and industry leadership networking capabilities.

4. **Consider smaller local companies or non-profit boards as stepping stones.** Some smaller local companies and non-profit boards may help a candidate gain entrée into for

profit boards or larger companies later. Some non-profit boards are comprised of for profit CEOs who can be a valuable resource. Choose carefully.

5. **Be realistic about the time available to commit to board service.** There are only 24 hours in a day. Be realistic as to how much time you have to be a contributing member of a board, especially if your current employment is more than full time.

6. **Establish a governance goal and ask for advice.** Board candidates should tell other executives and board members that they are interested in serving on a board of directors and ask those corporate insiders to make introductions to someone in their network.

7. **Network with current board members.** Attend events to network with board members in a position to make candidate recommendations to other board members.

8. **Consult the experts: board search consultants.** Schedule a private meeting with the board search consultant in your area. Visit **www.womenleadinghealthcare.org** to view a current list of board search experts known to WBL.

9. **Start the conversation about gender diversity in the boardroom.** Starting a conversation about gender diversity in the boardroom–while similar to stating your governance goal–can have several benefits such as increasing the number of board searches where gender diversity is considered and putting more women on the board's radar screen. Consider the following talking points:

Is there a businesswoman on your board of directors?

Yes

No

How many women are on the board?

Is the company actively searching for a new member?

A study has shown that three or more female board members make a crucial difference in governance and decision-making.

This 2006 study, *Critical Mass on Corporate Boards: Why Three or More Women Enhance Governance*, is published by the Wellesley Centers for Women and is available online for a fee.

Yes

No

Encourage the company to consider a woman when time comes to choose a new member.

Studies have shown that board processes differ, governance is improved, and return on equity is increased.

A 2007 Catalyst study, *The Bottom Line, Corporate Performance and Women on Boards*, highlights the potential increases in return on equity when additional women are on a company's board. This report is available on Catalyst's website.

Encourage the company to use outside resources for the board search. Outside resources can include both professional search firms and volunteer organizations like the WBL Foundation.

10. **Be an advocate for diversity in the boardroom.** Everyone has some type of relationship with a for profit corporation–as an owner, investor, employee, or even a consumer of the company's products or services. Consider who is on those companies' board of directors, and use your research and inquisitiveness to make the topic of boardroom diversity a priority.

How can boards find women director candidates?

The following are examples of organizations that work with boards to increase diversity:

1. **Women Business Leaders of the U.S. Health Care Industry Foundation.** WBL works with any company's board or search firm. WBL announces the opportunity via the organization's e-mail list. The name of the company searching does not have to be disclosed. Interested potential candidates reply to WBL by email, and submit their resumes. WBL provides all resumes received to the requesting company. For more information, visit **www. womenleadinghealthcare.org**.

2. **Women Corporate Directors.** Women Corporate Directors is the only national community of Women Corporate Directors who meet for regional dinners, at national conferences, and are connected by email for updates, to distribute board opportunities and to conduct surveys. To learn more, visit **www.womencorporatedirectors.com**.

3. **Northwestern University's Kellogg School of Management's Center for Executive Women.** Established in June 2001 by the Kellogg School of Management, the Center for Executive Women's goal is to help more women advance to boardrooms. The Center offers several educational programs for businesswomen, and maintains a database of women pursuing Fortune 1000 board seats who have completed their programs. Visit **www.kellogg. northwestern.edu/research/cew/** to learn more.

4. **The Director's Council.** Founded in 2003 by eight experienced businesswomen, the Director's Council works as a search firm to recruit and retain excellent minority candidates for boards, including women. To learn more, visit **www.directorscouncil.com**.

5. **Boardroom Bound.** This non-profit organization works with companies to supply educated diversity candidates for board service. To learn more about Boardroom Bound's board search and educational opportunities, visit **www.boardroombound.biz**.

CHAPTER ELEVEN

Where Can Board Candidates and Board Members Find the Best Advice and the Best Practices?

Commentators, attorneys, and pundits have put forth dozens of best practices that a board and director may choose to follow. As mentioned throughout this book, each company is different, each board is different, and consequently, the best practices for a director serving each board will be different. Some sources of best practices are specifically targeted toward a single problem. For example, Richard P. Kusserow, President of Strategic Management Systems, Inc. and former Inspector General of HHS, recently published a book entitled *49 Steps to Implement Sarbanes-Oxley Best Practices in Private and Nonprofit Health Care Entities.*[184]

There are numerous best practices from which to choose. The challenge for any director is to choose and implement the ones appropriate for his or her situation and company. Choosing the right best practices is important—they are not window dressing. Instead, best practices should become the fabric of how a board's business, and how the company's business, gets done. Choosing best practices also is a dynamic process that requires reassessment and updating as this area of the law changes periodically as a result of changes in legislation, case law and research in the field.

Due Diligence, Before Saying "Yes"

As you have read throughout this book, one of the first best practices is for a board candidate to perform due diligence before accepting any position on a board of directors. The days of just saying "yes" are over. The company's senior management and current board members will be conducting a due diligence process to determine whether to extend an offer to a particular board candidate. So, too, should the candidate ask questions to make sure that there is a desired match. This is critically important given that board membership requires a close and personal relationship amongst the directors and with senior management.

In that regard, a director candidate may want to consider the following due diligence steps before accepting a board directorship:

+ Collect and review as much information as possible about the company, paying particular attention to the following areas:

  ✧ the amount and frequency of litigation against the company;

  ✧ changes in the outside auditors of the company;

  ✧ press stories about the company;

  ✧ turnover in the senior management or membership of the board; and

  ✧ management letters from outside auditors if available (subject to the company's confidentiality policies).

+ Ask about the frequency and location of board meetings to determine convenience and likelihood of attendance.

+ Interview current board members, senior management, and former board members to determine the corporate culture for attendance and decision-making.

- ✦ Inquire about self-evaluation tools used by the board, toward understanding board commitment to high standards in governance.

- ✦ Review (or have reviewed) the company's risk management tools for director liability by paying particular attention to the following areas:

  - ✧ the company's indemnification provisions in its articles and bylaws;

  - ✧ the applicable sections of the business corporation act of the state in which the company is incorporated;

  - ✧ the duties of the board members as described in the bylaws and roles of the company's officers and committees; and

  - ✧ the coverage provided by the company's D&O insurance policy, recent premium history, and changes to the company's D&O insurance policy.

- ✦ Gain comfort about the existence and effectiveness of the company's corporate compliance program and/or code of conduct.

The last item listed above is particularly important for those companies that do business with the federal (and some state) governments. For example, if a company has a Medicare or Medicaid receivable, or if the company sells products covered by such government programs, a board member may want to make sure that the company's corporate compliance program includes adequate provisions specific to the risks of doing business with these federal and state health care programs.[185]

Best Practices for the Incumbent Director

In addition to the preliminary actions a board candidate may want to take before accepting a board opportunity, the board member also may wish to consider the roles he or she intends to assume once he or she is a board member. One should strive to be an *effective* board member, not just a board member.

Director Training Programs

A board member may wish to seek out additional training to become a more effective director. In July 2002, the Kellogg School of Management at Northwestern University opened its Center for Executive Women and hosted its inaugural Women Director Development Conference for women executives. The purpose of the Conference is to train current and future women directors to be more effective.[186] Stanford University Graduate School of Business, along with Stanford Law School, hosts a Stanford Directors' Forum. The program explores how directors can "best represent shareholders and other stakeholders in their advising and oversight roles," and "provides strategies to understanding the current governance environment."[187] A number of other business schools and universities are creating similar programs.

Membership organizations can be a valuable source of training as well. The National Association of Corporate Directors provides a multitude of training programs for any director interested in furthering his or her knowledge.[188] Women Corporate Directors holds "mini-conferences" lasting approximately half a day that highlight key issues related to being or becoming a board member.

Board members also may seek out consultants or experts to assist the board with complex and detailed legal and regulatory issues, especially when new regulations and standards impact roles of board members. For example, Susan F. Shultz, founder of SSA Executive Search International, provides several options for director education including a service to help the board complete self-evaluations.[189] Other similar programs are available throughout the United States.

In any event, the best defense against the pitfalls of serving as a board member, quite simply, is to be a conscientious board member.

Self Evaluation Tools

As discussed in more detail in Chapter Six, the NYSE requires the boards of directors of all listed companies to conduct self evaluations on a regular basis. Regardless of whether a company is listed on the NYSE, self evaluation tools are very useful to ensure that the board and its committees are functioning properly and highlight areas for improvement.

Although each board should tailor its self evaluation tool to the particular facts and circumstances of the board and the company, board self evaluation tools typically include factors to be rated from very good to poor, such as:

✦ "Board has full and common understanding of the roles and responsibilities of a board.

✦ Board members understand the organization's mission and its products/programs.

✦ Structural pattern (Board, officers, committees, executive, and staff) is clear.

✦ Board has clear goals and actions resulting from relevant and realistic strategic planning.

✦ Board receives regular reports on finances/budges, products/program performance and other important matters.

✦ Board meetings facilitate focus and progress on important organizational matters.

✦ Board regularly evaluates and develops the chief executive.

✦ Each member of the board feels involved and interested in the Board's work.

✦ All necessary skills and stakeholders and diversity are represented on the board."[190]

Best Practices to Support Women Directors

In a gender diverse boardroom, men can contribute to the successful participation of women, and therefore to the success of the board, itself. Consider the following list, which was taken from the Wellesley Centers for Women's 2006 Report:

+ "Be sure that a woman's comments are heard; if the conversation goes on as though the woman has not spoken, reinforce what she has said and give her credit for it.

+ If you notice a woman being ignored or slighted, let her know you see what is happening and then make it clear to others that you don't view this as acceptable board behavior.

+ Be aware of informal occasions (golf for example) where women directors are not present and board business is discussed.

+ Find time and ways to get to know the women informally to the same extent that you get to know the other men.

+ Don't expect women to raise gender and diversity issues by themselves; be alert to those issues and take initiative to raise them also.

+ Don't get suspicious that women are conspiring when women are seen talking or sitting together.

+ Put women on nominating committees.

+ Ask women, not only those on the nominating committee, to suggest women board candidates.

+ Point out to the board that having one or two women is not enough.

+ Insist that search firms and nominating committees provide diverse slates of board candidates."[191]

Commentary from the Experts

From *BusinessWeek* to Alan Greenspan, leading experts give commentary on best practices for corporate governance. Each expert has his or her own list of ideas for the essential characteristics of a conscientious board member. These comments serve as guiding principles for any person board candidate or member. Although many of these suggestions may seem obvious and grounded in common sense, a director who takes these suggestions to heart is likely to serve his or her company well.

Business Week *Survey*

In its October 7, 2002 issue, *Business Week* published its survey, *The Best and Worst Boards—How the corporate scandals are sparking a revolution in governance.* The year-long study polled the "nation's top governance experts" and conducted a detailed analysis of each board's performance records, noting everything from attendance records to stock ownership of individual board members. Among other things, the study reported that "a corporate governance revolution was underway," and that "directors whose main contribution to boardroom debate had been golf scores and gossip are returning to the classroom to learn how to read a balance sheet." [192]

The survey based its analysis of each board on the following basic criteria, identified by governance experts as indicia of a good corporate for profit board comprised of good directors:

+ *"Independence.* No more than two directors should be current or former company executives, and none should do business with the company or accept consulting or legal fees from it. The audit, compensation and nominating committees should be made up solely of independent directors." [193]

+ *"Stock Ownership.* Each director should own an equity stake in the company worth at least $150,000, excluding stock options. The only exception: new board members who haven't had time to build a large stake."[194]

✦ *"Director Quality*. Boards should include at least one independent director with experience in the company's core business and one who is the CEO of an equivalent sized company. Fully employed directors should sit on no more than four boards, retirees no more than seven. Each director should attend at least 75% of all meetings."[195]

✦ *"Board Activism*. Boards should meet regularly without management present and should evaluate their own performance every year. Audit committees should meet at least four times a year. Boards should be frugal on executive pay, decisive when planning a CEO succession, diligent in oversight responsibilities, and quick to act when trouble strikes."[196]

Dorothy Light and Katie Pushor

Dorothy Light and Katie Pushor reported the results of their research on the characteristics of a good director in their book, *Into the Boardroom*. They asked CEOs and directors to share their observations on "what distinguishes the exceptional directors from those who simply keep their chair pad warm.... Two characteristics generated widespread agreement: the ability to work well with the other members of the board and financial acumen."[197]

Corporate Board Member

In its January/February 2003 issue, *Corporate Board Member* presented an interview conducted by Rob Norton entitled *Ethics: Don't Leave Home Without Them*. Mr. Norton interviewed James A. Mitchell, the retired executive vice president of American Express Co. and former chairman and CEO of IDS Life, the nation's 14th largest life insurance company. In the interview, Mr. Mitchell expressed his belief that ethics in business *begins* with the ethics of the board members of a company. He said "Sure, the CEO is responsible for recommending things like the mission and values statements to the board. But it is the board's responsibility to see that those aren't just nice words on coffee cups."[198]

Susan F. Shultz

Susan F. Shultz identified no less than 23 distinguishing characteristics of a good director. Each one of these characteristics is explored in wonderful detail in her book, *The Board Book*:[199]

1. Keep the focus.
2. Be creative.
3. Prioritize ethics and values.
4. Avoid group think.
5. Know the business.
6. Support management.
7. Prepare.
8. Be positive.
9. Attend meetings.
10. Create an atmosphere of accountability.
11. Listen well.
12. Ask the right questions.
13. Maintain a good bedside manner.
14. Don't micromanage.
15. Be a coach.
16. Contribute.
17. Think full time job.
18. Be willing to take a position.
19. Limit the number of directorships.
20. Set priorities.

21. Exercise independence.

22. Be a catalyst to action.

23. Be willing to disagree.

Former Chairman Greenspan

Former Federal Reserve Chairman Alan Greenspan weighed in on the topic of corporate governance in his remarks on March 26, 2002 at the Stern School of Business, New York University. At the end of his speech he said:

> *Before concluding, I should like to emphasize that a market economy requires a structure of formal rules—a law of contracts, bankruptcy statutes, a code of shareholder rights—to name but a few. But rules cannot substitute for character. In virtually all transactions, whether with customers or with colleagues, we rely on the work of those with whom we do business. If we could not do so, goods and services could not be exchanged efficiently.*
>
> *Companies run by people with high ethical standards arguably do not need detailed rules to act in the long-run interests of shareholders and, presumably, themselves. But, regrettably human beings come as we are–some with enviable standards, but others who continually seek to cut corners. Yet there can be only one set of rules for corporate governance, and it must apply to all. Crafting the rules to provide the proper mix of regulatory and market-based incentives and penalties has never been easy. And I suspect that even after we get past the Enron debacle, crafting and updating such rules will continue to be a challenge.[200]*

SEC Chairman Cox

In a speech addressed on June 26, 2006 to the Stanford Law School Directors College, the newly appointed Chairman of the SEC, Christopher Cox, used an apt analogy when describing the current landscape for board members in serving their respective companies and their shareholder constituencies:

[T]oday, more than 50% of Americans own stocks, directly or through mutual funds and retirement plans. And now, as defined benefit pension plans give way to defined contribution plans, even more Americans will be taking charge of their investment decisions. And that means that even more Americans will be asking hard questions, and making demands.

Not too long ago, I read about a couple with a large family whose youngest son had never spoken. The boy was five years old. Then, one day, at breakfast, from out of the blue, the boy pushed his plate toward his mother and announced in perfect diction: "The eggs are cold."

The parents were flabbergasted. "What!?"

"I said...the eggs are cold."

The father raised his arms to heaven and repeated over and over, "He can talk! My son can talk!" The boy gave him a funny look and said, "Of course I can talk." And his father, who couldn't believe any of this, said, "Well then why, after five years, have you just now said something?"

And the boy said, "Because I'm a very patient sort. But finally, after all those years of cold eggs, I just couldn't take it any longer."

That investors are now speaking up may come as the same kind of a shock to directors as it did to those parents. If it ever were true that the corporation meant only management, and the shareholders were just silent partners along for the ride, that day is past.

Times are changing. We're in a new age of information and disclosure. If the eggs are cold, you're gonna hear about it.[201]

CLOSING REMARKS

We hope this book has provided you with brief answers to some of the frequently asked questions about serving as a board member. Obviously, much more information is available on this very important subject. Whether you are considering a directorship or currently serving in that capacity, we urge to seek out as much information as possible about effective board service. Stay current on new developments, as this is a dynamic area. For the informed person, the rewards should significantly outweigh the risks, which can be reduced if managed properly.

In closing, we trust that this book, combined with information you seek from other resources, will encourage more of you to "Answer the Call" for corporate board service.

Lynn Shapiro Snyder   Robert D. Reif

August 2007

ABOUT THE PUBLISHER

Women Business Leaders of the U.S. Health Care Industry Foundation™

The WBL Foundation is a non-profit organization exclusively dedicated to senior executive women and women board members who work in or with the health care industry. Unlike trade associations or other women's organizations, WBL provides a forum for these senior executive women and women board members in the health care industry to network exclusively with other senior executive women from across all segments of the health care industry. This includes manufacturers, payers, providers, and service providers to the health care industry. To date, more than 1,600 senior executive women and women board members participate in WBL. WBL's Foundation Associates participate by invitation only. WBL relies on an annual Summit and various sponsorships to fund its year long activities.

WBL's Mission Statement

The mission of the WBL Foundation is to help senior executive women and women board members in the health care industry improve their businesses and continue to grow professionally. The objectives to achieve that goal are the following:

+ facilitate networking opportunities for senior executive women and women board members in the health care industry;

+ increase the visibility of senior executive women and women board members in the health care industry;

+ expand the number of senior executive women in the health care industry; and

✦ increase the number of senior executive women from the health care industry who serve as a member of a board of directors.

Visit WBL's web site at **www.womenleadinghealthcare.org** or contact WBL at 202-955-7181 for more information.

ABOUT THE CONTRIBUTING COMPANIES

Darwin Professional Underwriters, contributing Authors of Chapter Four

Darwin is a specialty insurance group based in Farmington, Connecticut. The company is focused on the professional liability insurance market and underwrites directors & officers (D&O) liability for public and private companies, errors and omissions (E&O) liability insurance, and medical malpractice liability insurance. Darwin member companies include Darwin Professional Underwriters, Inc., Darwin National Assurance Company (DNA) and Darwin Select Insurance Company (DSI). Visit their website at **www.darwinpro.com**.

Epstein Becker & Green, P.C., founding sponsor of WBL

Founded in 1973, Epstein Becker & Green, P.C. (EBG) is a national law firm with a boutique approach to five complementary areas of practice. EBG's focus is on the core practice areas of:

+ Business Law

+ Health Care and Life Sciences

+ Labor and Employment

+ Litigation

+ Real Estate

EBG has one of the largest health care and life sciences practices in the United States.

Epstein Becker and Green's commitment to these practices reflects its founders' belief in focused proficiency paired with seasoned experience. Each practice is comprised of teams of experienced attorneys with the flexibility to take on cases of all sizes, and the mandate to deliver truly professional services.

EBG's core practices regularly share and access each other's knowledge and resources to provide clients with tailored solutions to their legal business issues. Understanding the complex evolution and critical trends within these areas enables EBG practitioners to provide clients with focused insight and deliver high quality service and results.

The firm has approximately 380 attorneys practicing in eleven offices throughout the U.S.–Atlanta, Chicago, Dallas, Houston, Los Angeles, Miami, New York, Newark, San Francisco, Stamford and Washington D.C. and law firm affiliates worldwide. The firm's website is located at **www.ebglaw.com**.

ABOUT THE AUTHORS

Lynn Shapiro Snyder, Esq.

Founder and President
Women Business Leaders of the U.S.
Health Care Industry Foundation, and
Senior Member
Epstein Becker & Green, P.C.

1227 25th Street, NW, Suite 700
Washington, D.C. 20037

Phone: (202) 861-1806
Fax: (202) 296-2882

LSnyder@ebglaw.com

Lynn Shapiro Snyder is the Founder and President of the
Women Business Leaders of the U.S. Health Care Industry
Foundation ("WBL Foundation"). See **www.
womenleadinghealthcare.org**. Ms. Snyder founded this 501 (c)
(3) non profit organization in 2001, with founding sponsor
Epstein Becker & Green, P.C., in order to meet the unmet needs
of senior executive women in the U.S. health care industry. The
mission of the Foundation is to help senior executive women in
the health care industry improve their businesses and continue
to grow professionally, through increased networking opportunities and by expanding the number of these senior executive
women who serve as a member of a board of directors.

Through Ms. Snyder's efforts, the Foundation has held several
successful Summits (the Foundation's major annual networking event), and Ms. Snyder has grown the Foundation from a
select group of 40 to include a network of over 1,600 senior
executive women and women board members–both in the
United States and abroad–who do business with the U.S.
health care industry. In addition, Ms. Snyder and the WBL

Foundation have assisted with many board searches, successfully having WBL Foundation Associates placed on these boards of directors, both for profit and non-profit.

Her efforts to foster "Horizontal Advancement™" of these senior executive women have made Ms. Snyder a nationally recognized speaker on the topics of corporate governance and gender diversity in the boardroom. She is co-author of this book, including two prior editions. Thousands of copies of the prior editions of "Answering the Call" have been distributed to executives in many different industries. She also is the author of a second book about best practices for vertical and horizontal advancement™ of women in business.

Ms. Snyder's role as Founder of the WBL Foundation has earned her national media attention. In 2007, she was named a "Woman to Watch" by Jewish Women International. In August 2002, *Modern Healthcare* magazine named Ms. Snyder as one of the "100 Most Powerful People in Healthcare" in its inaugural list. In April 2005, Modern Healthcare magazine named Ms. Snyder as one of the "Top 25 Women in Healthcare."

In addition to founding the WBL Foundation, Ms. Snyder is a senior member of the law firm, Epstein Becker & Green, P.C. Ms. Snyder serves on the firm's Board and Finance Committee. The law firm has one of the largest health care and life sciences practices in the United States. Ms. Snyder has almost thirty years of experience at the firm advising clients about federal, state, and international health law issues, including Medicare, Medicaid, TriCare, compliance, and managed care issues. She chairs the Third Party Payment Group and co-chairs the Health Care Fraud Practice Group. Her clients include health care providers, payors, pharmaceutical/device manufacturers and those companies and financial services firms that support the health care industry. She is a frequent speaker and publishes extensively. In the May 2006 issue of *Nightingale's Healthcare News*, Ms. Snyder was named one of the "Outstanding Fraud & Compliance Lawyers for 2006." In both the 2006 and 2007 editions of *The Best Lawyers* in America, Ms. Snyder was listed in the specialty of Health Care Law. She also has been quoted in the *New York Times* and other leading publications. Ms. Snyder's experience includes:

✦ Serving as lead defense counsel for several health care firms, including one of the largest pharmaceutical firms, one of the largest home health service firms, and one of the largest respiratory services firms in connection with significant fraud investigations/settlements with the federal and state governments;

✦ Representing several private equity investment banking firms regarding health regulatory compliance issues for large health care firm transactions including lead health regulatory counsel for the buyout of HCA by three private equity firms;

✦ Previously serving as outside General Counsel for over a decade to the American Managed Care and Review Association, one of the national trade associations for HMOs, PPOs, and UROs.

With respect to Ms. Snyder's international law activities, she has attended five health care business missions—Belgium 1995, Israel 1997, Brazil 1999, Italy 2002, Argentina 2005 and the Czech Republic 2006. She visited Israel in 2007 on a WBL Foundation business mission. She was board recertified as a Specialist in Health Law in the State of Florida for the period August 1, 2003-July 31, 2008.

Ms. Snyder represented several health trade associations during the enactment of the 1977 Medicare Anti-Fraud and Abuse Amendments and the 1978 HMO Amendments. Ms. Snyder has served as a member of: (1) the State of Florida Agency for Health Care Administration Health Care Fraud and Abuse Working Group (1993-1994); and (2) the Study Panel on Reforming the Fee-for-Service Medicare Program, sponsored by the National Academy of Social Insurance (1996-1998).

Ms. Snyder joined Epstein Becker & Green in 1979 and is admitted to practice law in the District of Columbia, the State of Florida, and before the United States Supreme Court. She earned a B.A. in Economics from Franklin & Marshall College in 1976 and her J.D. from the George Washington University National Law Center in 1979. On a more personal note, Ms. Snyder is married to Jeffrey M. Snyder and has three children, Rachel, Isaac, and Eitan. She resides in the Washington, D.C. area.

See **www.ebglaw.com** for additional information about the law firm and for a more detailed biography of Lynn Shapiro Snyder.

Current and Former Board Positions:

Board member, Founder, Women Business Leaders of the U.S. Health Care Industry Foundation

Board member, Trustmark Mutual Holding Company

Board member, Epstein Becker & Green, P.C.

Advisory Board, Washington Institute for Israel Health Policy Research

Advisory Board, Academy for International Health Studies

Advisory Board, BNA Health Care Fraud Reporter

Advisory Board, Protocare Sciences

Education:

J.D., George Washington University National Law Center, 1979

A.B., Franklin & Marshall College, 1976, Phi Beta Kappa, Magna Cum Laude—Major: Economics/Health Economics

Memberships:

American Bar Association, Health Care White Collar Crime Committee

American Health Lawyers Association

Benjamin Rush Society, Franklin & Marshall College, Advisory Council

Health on Wednesday, a group of Women Health Policy Experts, Founding Member

Women Business Leaders of the U.S. Health Care Industry Foundation

Robert D. Reif, Esq.

Chair, National Business Law Practice
Epstein Becker & Green, P.C.

1227 25th Street, NW, Suite 700
Washington, D.C. 20037

Phone: (202) 861-1829
Fax: (202) 296-2882

RReif@ebglaw.com

Robert D. Reif is a member of the Epstein Becker & Green, P.C.'s Health Care and Life Sciences Practice in the firm's Washington, DC office. Additionally, he chairs the firm's National Business Law Practice, and heads the Corporate and Transactions subgroup in the Washington, DC office, specializing in all aspects of corporate and transactional law for the health care industry, including mergers and acquisitions and other financings, conversion of nonprofit corporations to corporations for-profit, obtaining state and federal certifications, provider contract negotiation and product development implementation.

Mr. Reif represents a variety of health care companies, including managed care organizations, hospitals, insurance and pharmaceutical companies, physician groups, managed mental health care companies, prepaid dental plan companies, preferred provider organizations and utilization review companies.

Mr. Reif:

✦ Advises clients with regard to corporate structure, mergers and acquisitions, joint ventures, tax issues, including nonprofit tax exemption matters, contracting, licensing requirements, risk management and strategic planning

✦ Serves as lead transaction counsel in a variety of health care company transactions aggregating over $1 billion in value

✦ Advises companies, including venture capital companies, with regard to all aspects of the sales and acquisitions (non-hostile) of businesses

✦ Counsels companies seeking outside financing, including negotiating venture capital transactions, bank and other debt-financing transactions, private placement of securities under state and federal securities laws, corporate reorganizations, and corporate conversions from nonprofit to for-profit status.

Current and Former Board Positions:

Board Member, Epstein Becker & Green, P.C.

Education:

J.D., Catholic University of America, Columbus School of Law, 1977

B.A., University of Delaware, 1974

Memberships:

American Bar Association

American Health Lawyers Association

ABOUT THE AUTHORS
OF CHAPTER FOUR

Susan R. Chmieleski, APRN, CPHRM, FASHRM, JD
Vice President Risk Management and Client Services
Darwin Professional Underwriters
SChmieleski@darwinpro.com

As vice president for Darwin Professional Underwriters, Ms. Chmieleski is responsible for all client and risk management services. She develops programs and services for all insurance products and provides consulting and client services to policy-holders, helping them assess and manage their organizational risk. Ms. Chmieleski has written numerous comprehensive patient education tools and brochures, and is author to several published risk management articles. She has been a regular presenter at the American Society of Healthcare Risk Management annual conference and other regional meetings.

Ms. Chmieleski obtained a BS degree, summa cum laude, from the University of Hartford. She earned her JD degree from the University of Connecticut School of Law, where she was editor-in-chief of the Connecticut Insurance Law Journal. Ms. Chmieleski holds a Connecticut Nursing License, is a board-certified Advanced Practice Registered Nurse, and a Certified Professional in Healthcare Risk Management. She is licensed to practice law in Connecticut.

Cynthia Oard
Vice President, Health Care Underwriting
Darwin Professional Underwriters
COard@darwinpro.com

Ms. Oard leads Darwin's health care underwriting unit and is responsible for the management of the company's health care lines of business, including strategic product development and underwriting production.

With a multi-disciplinary team, including claims, risk management, and actuarial professionals, she manages a profitable portfolio of health care business.

Ms. Oard has over 20 years of underwriting experience in the area of health care management liability (directors and officers liability) and managed care errors and omissions. She joined Darwin following a long tenure with Chubb Specialty Insurance (formerly Executive Risk) where she served as the Midwest Region Underwriting Manager, and most recently as the New York Brokerage & Northern Health Care Zone Manager overseeing the underwriting and distribution of Health Care D&O and Managed Care E&O products. Ms. Oard was an integral member of the team that developed Executive Risk's entry into the managed care market, and has been a featured speaker at many industry associations including the Healthcare Financial Manager Association, Professional Liability Underwriting Society (PLUS) and the American Hospital Association.

ENDNOTES

[1] National Association of Corporate Directors, *2005 Public Company Governance Survey*, 22 (2005).

[2] Russell Reynolds Associates, *2000-2001 Board Practices Survey, The Structure and Compensation of Boards of Directors of U.S. Public Companies*, 24 (2001).

[3] Dorothy Light & Katie Pushor, *Into the Boardroom*, 4 (2002).

[4] *See, e.g.*, Model Bus. Corp. Act, § 8.30(a) (2002 Supplement). State law determines specific requirements for board members.

[5] *See, e.g.*, Model Nonprofit Corp. Act, § 8.30(a) (1987). State law determines specific requirements for board members.

[6] *See, e.g.*, Model Bus. Corp. Act, §§ 8.30(d) and 8.30(e) (2002 Supplement). State law determines specific requirements for board members.

[7] *Id.*

[8] *See, e.g.*, Corporate Fraud Task Force, *Second Year Report to the President*, 2.3 (2004).

[9] Bernard Black, Brian Cheffins & Michael Klausner, Outside Director Liability, *Stanford Law Review*, 1055 (February 2006).

[10] Fletcher Cyc. Corp., § 1041.10, 54. *See also* Stepak v. Addison, 20 F.3d 398 (11th Cir. 1994).

[11] Emily A. Moseley & Hayden J. Silver, III, *Building a Strong Board of Directors/Advisors & Board Best Practices Primer*, under Personal Liability of Board Members, *3 (2001)*.

[12] Fletcher Cyc. Corp., *supra* note 10, 55. *See also* Stepak v. Addison, 20 F.3d 398 (11th Cir. 1994).

13 Fletcher Cyc. Corp., *supra* note 10, 58. *See also* Model Business Corporation Act (1984).

14 Moseley & Silver, *supra* note 11.

15 Paula Desio, *An Overview of the United States Sentencing Commission and the Organizational Guidelines, available at* http://www.ussc.gov/TRAINING/corpover.PDF (last visited August 8, 2007).

16 Caremark International Inc. Derivative Litigation, 698 A. 2d 959 (Del.Ch. 1996).

17 *Id.* at 970.

18 *Id.* at 969.

19 *Id.* at 969-970.

20 *Id.* at 971.

21 *In re* The Walt Disney Co. Deriv. Litig., 906 A.2d 27 (Del. 2006).

22 *Id.* at 67.

23 Jesse A. Finkelstein et al., Times May Change, But Fiduciary Duties Do Not: The Post-Trial Opinion in Disney, *Corporation*, 1, 7 (February 1, 2006).

24 The Securities and Exchange Commission, *About the SEC, The Laws That Govern the Securities Industry*, 1, *available at* http://www.sec.gov/about/laws.shtml (last visited August 9, 2007).

25 *Id.* at 2.

26 *Id.*

27 Moseley & Silver, *supra* note 11, 1.

28 Louis Lavelle, The Best and Worst Boards, How the Corporate Scandals are Sparking a Revolution in Governance, *Business Week, available at* http://www.businessweek.com (October 7, 2002) (last visited August 9, 2007).

29 Fletcher Cyc. Corp., § 900.15, 402, note 1. *See also* Reliance Elec. Co. v. Emerson Elec., 404 U.S. 418 (1972).

30 Pub. L. No. 107-204, 116 Stat. 745.

31 Moseley & Silver, *supra* note 11.

32 Fletcher Cyc. Corp., §1344.10, 562. *See also* King v. Gibbs, 876 F.2d 1275 (7th Cir. 1989).

33 Moseley & Silver, *supra* note 11, 2.

34 Fletcher Cyc. Corp., § 5432, 58. *See also* EBS Litigation LLC v. Barclays Global Investors, N.A., 304 F.3d 302 (3d Cir. 2002).

35 Fletcher Cyc. Corp., *supra* note 34, 59. *See also* Aiken v. Insull, 122 F.2d 746 (7th Cir. 1941), cert. den. 315 U.S. 806 (1942).

36 33 U.S.C. § 1251 et seq. (2000).

37 The Comprehensive Environmental Response, Compensation, and Liability Act (CERCLA), also known as Superfund, involves treatment and release of hazardous waste. *See* **http://www.epa.gov/superfund/ action/law/cercla.htm** for more information.

38 Fletcher Cyc. Corp., § 1234.24, 343, note 4. *See also* United States v. USX Corp., 68 F3d 811 (CA3 1995).

39 Moseley & Silver, *supra* note 11.

40 Fletcher Cyc. Corp., § 1264, 369, note 2. *See also* Vinick v. C.I.R., 110 F.3d 168 (1st Cir. 1997).

41 I.R.C. § 4958; Treas. Reg. § 53.4958-6.

42 29 U.S.C. § 1001 et seq. (2000).

43 U.S. Department of Labor, *Employee Retirement Income Security Act—ERISA, available at* **http://www.dol.gov/dol/ topic/health-plans/erisa.htm** (last visited September 4, 2007).

[44] Fletcher Cyc. Corp., § 6753, 325, note 4. *See also* 29 U.S.C. § 1002 (21).

[45] *Id.* at 326. *See also* 29 U.S.C. § 1109 (21).

[46] John R. Engen, What Are Your Chances of Going to Jail?, *Corporate Board Member*, Special Legal Issue, *available at* http://www.boardmember.com (2002) (last visited January 16, 2003).

[47] *Id.* at 1.

[48] *Id.* at 1.

[49] *Id.* at 2.

[50] *Id.*

[51] Black, Cheffins & Klausner, *supra* note 9.

[52] *Id.*

[53] *Id.* at 1056.

[54] Engen, *supra* note 46.

[55] Black, Cheffins & Klausner, *supra* note 9, 1056.

[56] Stewart M. Landefeld, Andrew B. Moore & Katherine Ann Ludwig, Eds., *The Public Company Handbook, A Practical Guide for Directors and Executives,* 120 (May 2002).

[57] *Id.*

[58] David M. Gische & Vicki E. Fishman, Ross Dixon & Bell, LLP, *Directors and Officers Insurance Liability,* 1, (2000).

[59] *Id.* at 2.

[60] *Id.* at 2.

[61] Towers Perrin, *Directors and Officers Liability—2006 Survey of Insurance Purchasing and Claims Trends,* 10, *available at* www.towersperrin.com/tp/getwebcachedoc?webc=HRS/USA/2007/200704/DO_Survey_Report2006_040507.pdf (last visited September 17, 2007).

[62]   Gerald Griffith, Michael Peregrine, Ralph DeJong, Paul DeMuro, Daniel Hale, David Hillman, Louise Joy, Shannon Kelley, John Libby, Gerald McGovern, Cynthia Reaves, & James Schwartz, Esqs., *Lessons for Healthcare from Enron: A Best Practices Handbook*, 149 (2002).

[63]   Stephen Taub, *D&O Insurance Prices Soften, Survey Says*, CFO.com, (January 27, 2006), *available at* **http://www.cfo.com** (last visited September 17, 2007).

[64]   David Stickney, Fewer Securities Class Actions Filed in 2006, *Institutional Investor Advocate*, *available at* **http://www. blbglaw.com/publications/2007lQStickneyFewCases2006. pdf** (last visited September 17, 2007).

[65]   John E. Black, Jr. & David T. Burrowes. IRMI, *D&O Litigation Trends in 2006* (May 2007).

[66]   *Id.* at 10.

[67]   Gische & Fishman, *supra* note 58.

[68]   *Id.*

[69]   Moseley & Silver, *supra* note 11 at 2.

[70]   Gische & Fishman, *supra* note 58 at 8.

[71]   *Id.*

[72]   Pub. L. No. 107-204, 116 Stat. 745.

[73]   148 Cong. Rec. S7365 (July 25, 2002).

[74]   148 Cong. Rec. H5480 (July 25, 2002).

[75]   Management's Report on Internal Control over Financial Reporting and Certifications of Disclosure in Exchange Act Periodic Reports, Final Rule, Securities Release No. 8392, Exchange Act Release No. 49313 (Feb. 4, 2004), 69 Fed. Reg. 9722 (March 1, 2004).

76   These rules became effective on August 5, 2003. Imple-
     mentation of Standards of Professional Conduct for
     Attorneys, Securities Release No. 8185, Exchange Act
     Release No. 47,276, (January 29, 2003), 68 Fed. Reg. 6296
     (February 6, 2003).

77   Certifications of Disclosure in Companies' Quarterly and
     Annual Reports, Securities Release No. 33-8124, Exchange
     Act Release No. 46,427 (Aug. 29, 2002), 67 Fed. Reg.
     57276 (September 9, 2002).

78   15 U.S.C. § 78p (2007) (requiring directors, officers, and
     principal stockholders to file statements with the SEC).

79   Item 406, Regulation S-K, 17 C.F.R. § 229.406 (2003). *See
     also* Disclosure Required by Sections 406 and 407 of the
     Sarbanes-Oxley Act of 2002, Securities Release No. 8177,
     Exchange Act Release No. 47,235 (January 23, 2003), 68
     Fed. Reg. 5110 (January 31, 2003), *subsequent correction in*
     Securities Release No. 8177A, Exchange Act Release No.
     47,325A (March 26, 2003), 68 Fed. Reg. 15353
     (March 31, 2003).

80   Disclosure Required by Sections 406 and 407 of the
     Sarbanes-Oxley Act of 2002, Securities Release No. 8177,
     Exchange Act Release No. 47,235 (Jan. 23, 2003), 68 Fed.
     Reg. 5110. *See also* Item 5.05 of Form 8-K, 17 C.F.R. §
     249.308 (2003).

81   Sarbanes-Oxley Act § 806, 18 U.S.C. § 1514A (2002); *See
     generally* Allen B. Roberts, *The Sarbanes-Oxley Act: Employ-
     ment Implications for Privately Held and Publicly Traded
     Companies* (May 2006) *available at* **http://www.ebglaw.
     com/files/7310_article_800.htm** (last visited September
     28, 2007) (providing an overview of whistleblower protec-
     tion on both the federal and state levels).

82   Amy Borrus, *Learning to Love Sarbanes-Oxley,*
     BusinessWeek 126 (November 21, 2005).

83 Public Company Accounting Oversight Board, Order Approving Proposed Auditing Standard No. 2, *An Audit of Internal Control Over Financial Reporting Performed in Conjunction with an Audit of Financial Statements,* Exchange Act Release No. 49,884 (June 17, 2004) 69 Fed. Reg. 35083 (providing professional standards and guidance for independent auditors to attest to managements' reports on internal controls over financial reporting).

84 GAO, *Report to the Committee on Small Business and Entrepreneurship, U.S. Senate, Sarbanes-Oxley Act: Consideration of Key Principles Needed in Addressing Implementation for Smaller Public Companies,* at 17 (April 2006) *available at*: **http://www.gao.gov/new.items/d06361.pdf.**

85 Amendments to Rules Regarding Management's Report on Internal Control Over Financial Reporting, Securities Release No. 33-8809, Exchange Act Release No. 55928 (June 20, 2007), 72 Fed. Reg. 35310 (June 27, 2007).

86 *See* Final Rule: Additional Form 8-K Disclosure Requirements and Acceleration of Filing Date, Securities Release No. 8400, Exchange Act Release No. 49,424 (Mar. 25, 2004), 69 Fed. Reg. 15593 (March 25, 2004), *subsequent correction in* Securities Release No. 8400A, Exchange Act Release No. 49,424A, (August 4, 2004), 69 Fed. Reg. 48370 (August 10, 2004).

87 *Id.*

88 18 U.S.C. § 1513(e) (2002) (amending the obstruction of justice statute to include a prohibition against retaliation).

89 Implementation of Standards of Professional Conduct for Attorneys, Securities Release No. 8185, Exchange Act Release No. 47,276, (Jan. 29, 2003).

90 American Institute of Certified Public Accountants, *The State Cascade—An Overview of the State Issues Related to the Sarbanes-Oxley Act, available at* **www.aicpa.org** (last visited September 12, 2003).

[91] *See generally* NYSE Euronext, Overview (and related links) *available at* **http://www.nyse.com/about/history/1089312755484.html** (last visited September 1, 2007).

[92] Press Release, Scott Peterson, NASDAQ Marks 30th Anniversary, February 8, 2001, *available at* **www.nasdaq.com/Newsroom/news/pr2001/ne_section01_040.html** (last visited September 1, 2007).

[93] NASDAQ, *Overview: About the NASDAQ Stock Market, available at* **www.nasdaq.com/about/overview.stm** (last visited September 1, 2007).

[94] Self Regulatory Organizations; New York Stock Exchange, Inc. and National Association of Securities Dealers, Inc.; Order Approving Proposed Rule Changes (SR-NYSE-2002-33 and SR-NASD-2002-141) and Amendments No. 1 Thereto; Order Approving Proposed Rule Changes (SR-NASD-2002-77, SR-NASD-2002-80, SR-NASD-2002-138 and SR-NASD_2002-139) and Amendments No. 1 to SR-NASD-2002-80 and SR-NASD-2002-139; and Notice of Filing and Order Granting Accelerated Approval of Amendment Nos. 2 and 3 to SR-NYSE-2002-33, Amendment Nos. 2,3,4 and 5 to SR-NASD-2002-141, Amendment Nos. 2 and 3 to SR-NASD_2002-80, Amendment Nos. 1,2, and 3 to SR-NASD-2002-138, and Amendment No. 2 to SR-NASD-2002-139, Relating to Corporate Governance, 68 Fed. Reg. 64154 (2003).

[95] Commissioner Cynthia A. Glassman, *Speech by SEC Commissioner: Board Diversity: The 21ˢᵗ Century Challenge: "The New Regulatory Climate and Impact on Board Composition,"* U.S. Securities and Exchange Commission (November 11, 2005, New York, New York), *available at* **www.sec.gov/news/speech/spch111105cag.htm** (last visited September 1, 2007).

[96] NYSE, Section 303A: Corporate Governance Rules, *available at* **www.nyse.com/pdfs/section303A_final_rules.pdf** (last visited September 27, 2007) and NYSE, Listed Company Manual Section 303A: Frequently Asked Questions, *available at* **www.nyse.com/pdfs/section303Afaqs.pdf** (last visited September 27, 2007).

[97] The NASDAQ Stock Market, NASDAQ Corporate Governance Rules 4200, 4200A, 4350, 4350A, 4351, and 4360 and Associated Interpretative Material (April 15, 2004), *available at* **www.nasdaq.com/about/FAQsCorpGov.stm** (last visited September 27, 2007).

[98] NYSE, *supra* note 96.

[99] The NASDAQ Stock Market, *supra* note 97.

[100] Glassman, *supra* note 95.

[101] Abigail Arms, *Corporate Governance Practices of the 100 Largest U.S. Public Companies, in Corporate Governance 2005: Dealing with the Governance & Disclosure Challenges Ahead*, 2 (2005) (PLI course handbook).

[102] Spencer Stuart, 20th Annual Spencer Stuart Director Survey Shows Scope of Governance Changes (September 19, 2005) *available at* **www.spencerstuart.com/about/media/34/print/** (last visited March 23, 2006).

[103] *Id.*

[104] *Id.*

[105] *Id.*

[106] Evelyn Cruz Sroufe & Susan J. Naficy, Directors Assess Thyself: Board Self Evaluations, an Emerging Best Practice, *Corporation*, 1 (October 17, 2005).

[107] NYSE & NASD, *Report and Recommendations of the Blue Ribbon Committee on Improving the Effectiveness of Corporate Audit Committees*, (1999), *available at* **www.nasdaq.com/about/Blue_Ribbon_Panel.pdf** (last visited September 27, 2007).

[108] NYSE, The NASDAQ Stock Market, *supra* notes 96, 97.

[109] Fried, Frank, Harris, Shriver, & Jacobson, SEC Adopts Rules under the Sarbanes-Oxley Act of 2002 on Codes of Ethics and Audit Committee Financial Experts, (January 29, 2003) *available at* **www.friedfrank.com/cmemos/030129_codes_ of_ethics.htm** (last visited April 30, 2007).

[110] Claudia H. Deutsch, As Boards Regroup, More Women Join, *New York Times,* (December 1, 2002), *available at* **www. nytimes.com/ref/open/profiles/01EXLIOPEN.html**) (last visited August 9, 2007).

[111] *Id.*

[112] *Id.*

[113] *See generally,* United States Department of Health and Human Services, Office of Inspector General & American Health Lawyers Association, *An Integrated Approach to Corporate Compliance: A Resource for Health Care Organization Boards of Directors (Supplement to 2003 Publication)* (July 1, 2004).

[114] United States Department of Health and Human Services, Office of Inspector General & American Health Lawyers Association, *Corporate Responsibility and Corporate Compliance: A Resource for Health Care Boards of Directors* (2003); United States Department of Health and Human Services, Office of Inspector General & American Health Lawyers Association, *An Integrated Approach to Corporate Compliance: A Resource for Health Care Organization Boards of Directors (Supplement to 2003 Publication)* (July 1, 2004).

[115] James J. Fishman, Standards of Conduct for Directors of Non-profit Corporations, 7 *Pace Law Rev.* 442 (1987).

[116] IRC § 501(c)(3); Treas. Reg. § 1.501(a)-1(c).

[117] Internal Revenue Service, *Sample Conflicts of Interest Policy* (Revised 1999), *available at* **http://www.irs.gov/instructions/i1023/ar03.html** (last visited September 27, 2007).

[118] Queen of Angels Hospital v. Younger, 136 Cal. Rptr. 36 (Cal. Ct. App. 1977).

[119] Stern v. Lucy Webb Hayes National Training School for Deaconesses & Missionaries, 381 F. Supp 1003 (D.D.C. 1974).

[120] Rev. Ruling 69-545, 1969-2 C.B. 117.

[121] IRC § 501(c)(3).

[122] IRC § 511.

[123] *In re* Manhattan Eye, Ear and Throat Hosp., 715 N.Y.S. 2d 575 (1999).

[124] *Id*. at 593.

[125] IRC § 501(c)(3).

[126] *Id*.

[127] IRC § 4958(f)(1).

[128] IRC § 4958(c)(1).

[129] *See* Internal Revenue Service, Form 4720 Instructions, *available at* **http://www.irs.gov/pub/irs-pdf/i4720.pdf** (last visited December 11, 2005).

[130] IRC § 4958.

[131] IRC § 4958(a)(1).

[132] IRC § 4958(b).

[133] IRC § 4958 (a)(2).

[134] *See, e.g.* Tex. Civ. Prac. & Rem. § 84.

[135] ABA Coordinating Committee on Non-profit Governance, *Guide to Non-profit Corporate Governance in the Wake of Sarbanes-Oxley*, 2 (2005).

[136] *Id*.

137 Catalyst, The Prout Group, The Executive Leadership Council, and the Hispanic Association on Corporate Responsibility, *Women and Minorities on Fortune 100 Boards*, 2, (May 17, 2005), *available at* **http://www.catalyst. org** (last visited June 6, 2005).

138 U.S. Department of Education, National Center for Education Statistics, *Digest of Education Statistics*, NCES 2007-017, Table 251 (July 2007), *available at* **http:// nces.ed.gov/pubsearch/pubsinfo.asp?pubid=2005154** (last visited August 8, 2007).

139 The Calvert Group, Ltd., *Issue Brief: Board Diversity*, (April 4, 2006), *available at* **http://www.calvert.com/sri_ib_4.html**, (last visited April 4, 2006), quoting Business Women's Network, WOW! Quick Facts #4084, (Aug. 2004).

140 Catalyst, *2006 Catalyst Census of Women Board Directors of the Fortune 500*, (2006), *available at* **http://www.catalyst.org** (last visited August 8, 2007).

141 *Id.*

142 Wellesley Centers for Women, *Critical Mass on Corporate Boards: Why Three or More Women Enhance Governance*, 37 (2006).

143 *Id.* at 34.

144 Catalyst, *supra* note 140.

145 The Conference Board/Heidrick & Struggles, *Diversity on US Boards: Broadening the Profile of Corporate Boards*, (1998), *quoted in* Veronica J. Biggins, *The Corporate Board, Making Board Diversity Work*, 4 (July/August 1999).

146 Catalyst, *The Bottom Line: Connecting Corporate Performance and Women's Representation on Boards*, (2007), **http://www. catalyst.org/** (last visited October 2, 2007).

[147] David Carter, Betty Simkins & W. Gary Simpson, Corporate Governance, Board Diversity, and Firm Value, *The Financial Review*, Vol 38, p. 33-53 (2003).

[148] Catalyst, *supra*, note 146.

[149] Vanessa Anastapoulous, David Brown & Debra Brown, Women on Boards: Not Just the Right Thing...The Bright Thing, *Conference Board of Canada*, Cover (2002).

[150] *Id.*

[151] The NASDAQ Stock Market, *supra* note 97.

[152] Renee B. Adams & Daniel Ferreira, *European Corporate Governance Institute Working Paper, Gender Diversity in the Boardroom–Working Paper No. 57/2004* (November 2004), *available at* **http://papers.ssrn.com** (last visited April 11, 2006).

[153] Wellesley Centers for Women, *supra* note 142 at v.

[154] Andrew Blackman, Corporate Governance Efforts Pressure Companies to Diversify, *The Wall Street Journal,* *available at* **http://www.careerjournal.com** (last visited March 27, 2006).

[155] *Id.*

[156] Phred Dvorak, Breaking into the Boardroom, *The Wall Street Journal,* B3 (March 7. 2006).

[157] Biggins, *supra* note 145, 2.

[158] Catalyst, *supra* note 1440.

[159] Catalyst, *The Bottom Line: Connecting Corporate Performance and Gender Diversity*, 2 (2004), **http://www.catalyst.org/ knowledge/titles/title.php?page=lead_finperf_04** (last visited September 27, 2007).

[160] Dvorak, *supra* note 156.

[161] European Professional Women's Network, *Women on Boards: The Inside Story on Norway's 40% Target*, (April 4, 2006), available at **http://www.eurpoeanpwn.net/tht_wob/articles/story_on_norway.html** (last visited April 4, 2006).

[162] *Id.*

[163] Butigan, Ken, Chile Inaugurates First Woman to Serve as President, *New York Times*, (March 12, 2006), *available at* **http://www.nytimes.com** (last visited September 27, 2007).

[164] Office of State Treasurer Denise L. Nappier, Press Release: Nappier Initiative Promotes Independence, Diversity on Corporate Boards (October 21, 2002), *available at:* **http://www.state.ct.us/ott/pressreleases/press2002/pr101502.pdf** (last visited September 27, 2007).

[165] *Id.* at 3.

[166] Office of State Treasurer Denise Nappier, Bringing Diversity to the Boardroom: Connecticut's Unique Partnership, *available at* **http://www.state.ct.us/ott/pressreleases/press2002/ pr101502. pdf** (last visited August 2006).

[167] The Calvert Group, Ltd., Resolution Filing History, (2007), *available at* **http://www.calvertgroup.com/sri_6979.html** (last visited September 17, 2007).

[168] To see the Model Language, visit **http://www.calvert. com/pdf/boarddiv_model_charter.pdf**.

[169] Carter, Simkins & Simpson, *supra* note 147.

[170] *Id.*

[171] National Association of Corporate Directors, *2005 Public Governance Survey*, 2 (2005).

[172] Dennis C. Carey & Nayla Rizk, *Spencer Stuart Governance Letter: Seismic Shift in Board Competition*, (Third Quarter 2005).

[173] *Id.* at 38.

[174] Wellesley Centers for Women, *supra* note 142, 53.

[175] *Id.* at 49.

[176] Catalyst, *2006 Catalyst Census of Women Corporate Officers* (2006), *available at:* **http://www.catalyst.org** (last visited September 27, 2007).

[177] European Foundation for the Improvement of Living and Working Conditions, *Rules on Minimum Gender Representation on Company Boards Come into Force,* (April, 2004) *available at* **http://www.eiro.eurofound.eu. int/2006/02/feature/no0602102f.html** (last visited September 27, 2007.)

[178] Theodore Dysart, Board Trends for 2006: It's Back to the Future, *Heidrick & Struggles Governance Letter,* 63 (2005).

[179] Carey & Rizk, *supra* note 172.

[180] *Id.* at 38.

[181] Letter from Julie H. Daum to Lynn Shapiro Snyder, November 22, 2006.

[182] *Id.*

[183] Lynn Shapiro Snyder also is the author of the book *Advancing Women in Business: Ten Best Practices,* also published by the Women Business Leaders of the U.S. Health Care Industry Foundation in 2007. This book focuses on best practices for vertical advancement but focuses specifically on best practices for horizontal advancement,™ with a closer look at board placement.

[184] Richard P. Kusserow & Rita Kuyumcuoglu, *49 Steps to Implement Sarbanes-Oxley Best Practices,* (2006).

[185] United States Department of Health and Human Services, Office of Inspector General & American Health Lawyers Association, *An Integrated Approach to Corporate Compliance: A Resource for Health Care Organization Boards of Directors* (July 1, 2004); United States Department of Health and Human Services, Office of Inspector General & American Health Lawyers Association, *An Integrated Approach to Corporate Compliance: A Resource for Health Care Organization Boards of Directors (Supplement to 2003 Publication)* (July 1, 2004); United States Department of Health and Human Services, Office of Inspector General & American Health Lawyers Association, *Corporate Responsibility and Corporate Compliance: A Resource for Health Care Boards of Directors* (2003).

[186] For more information, *see* **http://www.kellogg.northwestern.edu/research/cew/**.

[187] For more information, *see* **http://www.gsb.stanford.edu/exed/sdf/index.html**.

[188] For information, *see* **http://www.nacdonline.org**.

[189] For a complete description of these services and programs, *see* **http://www.ssaexec.com**.

[190] Carter McNamara, *Field Guide to Developing and Operating Your Nonprofit Board of Directors* (2003).

[191] Wellesley Centers for Women, *supra* note 142, 51.

[192] Louis Lavelle, *supra* note 28.

[193] *Id.*

[194] *Id.*

[195] *Id.*

[196] *Id.*

[197] Light and Pushor, *supra* note 3, 49.

[198] Rob Norton, Ethics, Don't Leave Home Without Them, *Corporate Board Member* (January/February 2003) *available at*: **http://www.boardmember.com/issues/archive.pl?article_id=11325** (last visited September 28, 2007).

[199] Susan F. Schultz, *The Board Book*, 154-167 (2001).

[200] Alan Greenspan, *Corporate Governance*, Remarks by Chairman Alan Greenspan, Stern School of Business, New York University, N.Y., N.Y. (March 26, 2002).

[201] Christopher Cox, *Speech by SEC Chairman: Address to the Stanford Law School Directors' College* (June 26, 2006) *available at* **http://www.sec.gov/news/speech/2006/spch062606cc.htm** (last visited September 28, 2007).

WOMEN BUSINESS LEADERS
OF THE
U.S. HEALTH CARE INDUSTRY FOUNDATION™

WWW.WOMENLEADINGHEALTHCARE.ORG

PROMOTING *HORIZONTAL ADVANCEMENT*™

Order Additional Copies of Answering the Call:

Understanding the Duties, Risks, and Rewards of Corporate Governance

By Lynn Shapiro Snyder, Esq. and Robert D. Reif, Esq.

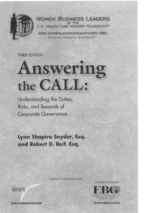

This book provides an overview of what one should consider as a member of a board of directors–including an overview of the various areas where a director may be held personally liable, what it means to be qualified for an audit committee, best practices for good corporate governance, and an in-depth look at D&O insurance written by the experts – representatives from a D&O insurance firm. All proceeds from this book benefit WBL.

This book also explores the benefits of gender diversity in the boardroom, in an effort to help men and women "Answer the Call" for board service.

+ 1 book: $24.95 per book plus shipping
+ 2-12 books: $21.95 per book plus shipping* (a "Board set")
+ 13 books or more: $19.95 per book plus shipping*

Books also can be purchased at www.womenleadinghealthcare.org

Answering the Call: Third Edition – Order Form

Your Name: _____

Your Title: _____

Your Company: _____

"Ship-to" Name & Address: _____

Your Phone Number: _____

Number of Copies & Total Amount: _____

Pay by sending this form to WBL via fax at (202) 861-3531 or email to Sonja Sadowski at ssadowski@ebglaw.com. You may pay by credit card only; WBL accepts Visa, MasterCard, and American Express, and your card will not be charged until the book is ready to be shipped. Any questions, contact WBL at (202) 955-7181. Please complete the following:

Name as it appears on Credit Card: _____

Credit Card Number: _____

Expiration Date: _____

Signature: _____

* For discount to be applicable, books must be bought simultaneously.

To order, remove this form by cutting here, or visit www.womenleadinghealthcare.org

WOMEN BUSINESS LEADERS
OF THE
U.S. HEALTH CARE INDUSTRY FOUNDATION™

WWW.WOMENLEADINGHEALTHCARE.ORG
PROMOTING HORIZONTAL ADVANCEMENT™

ORDER FORM
Advancing Women in Business:
10 BEST PRACTICES
with a special focus on board placement
By Lynn Shapiro Snyder

At the Inaugural WBL Summit in 2002, a group of about eighty senior executive women from the health care industry met in small groups to discuss their careers and their career advancement (both vertical and horizontal advancement™). These women collectively identified their most important wisdom and advice that they would give to other women looking to advance in business. This collective wisdom was used to form WBL's "Ten Best Practices for Advancing Women in Business." All proceeds from this book benefit WBL.

This book explores various ways to approach each of these ten best practices – with examples and action items. The book also examines ten best practices for making the board nominating committee's "radar screen" in order to gain corporate board seats – one of the core principles of horizontal advancement.™

$19.95 per book, plus shipping
Publication expected early 2008

Advancing Women in Business – Order Form

Your Name: _____

Your Title: _____

Your Company: _____

"Ship-to" Name & Address: _____

Your Phone Number: _____

Number of Copies & Total Amount: _____

Pay by sending this form to WBL via fax at (202) 861-3531 or email to Sonja Sadowski at ssadowski@ebglaw.com. For pre-sale, you may pay by credit card only; WBL accepts Visa, MasterCard, and American Express, and your card will not be charged until the book is ready to be shipped. Any questions, contact WBL at (202) 955-7181. Please complete the following:

Name as it appears on Credit Card: _____

Credit Card Number: _____

Expiration Date: _____

Signature: _____

To order, remove this form by cutting here, or visit www.womenleadinghealthcare.org